AFTER NORMAL

AFTER NORMAL

MAKING SENSE OF THE GLOBAL ECONOMY

Samuel Rines

ISBN-13: 9781974166190
ISBN-10: 1974166198

To Those Who Bought Me Books

ACKNOWLEDGEMENTS

Numerous people deserve credit for the better parts of this book. Zach Beck, *The National Interest*, and Cati Rines have been sources of inspiration and a great deal of help. Andrew Sprague made me publish my first op-ed. Dana and Lorraine Rines still have too many of my books at their house. Worth Wray reviewed many of the ideas in the book. And to everyone else, thank you.

CONTENTS

INTRODUCTION

In Remembrance of Normal

Blame for the Financial Crisis has been passed from politicians to Wall Street and back again. Banks have paid for their survival. But one more rehashing of the mundane facts of the Financial Crisis cannot add much to that discussion now. Moreover, the outcomes this book addresses are not, for the most part, contingent on the reasons for the crisis. This book probes instead what the economic and financial scars from that crisis will mean for the US and global economy, how the crisis has reshaped democracy, how it has changed monetary policy for the US and the world, and where the global economy may be heading next.

Parallels between the Great Depression and the Financial Crisis are frequently drawn. But there is a general failure to admit—or, more frighteningly, to understand—that the Depression was the impetus for pivotal, fundamental changes to the US economy and monetary policy mechanisms, changes sustained for nearly a century. Likewise, the Financial Crisis has brought fundamental change. "Creativity" is the new mantra of the Federal Reserve. The US is grappling with the "Uberization" of its economy and the profound impact of globalization. And liberal democracy is feeling its way through debt crises. The repercussions of excessive debt and experimental central bank interventions will be felt more potently and for longer than most forecasters are willing to admit. The Federal Reserve's balance sheet stands today at more than $4 trillion. And unwinding the balance sheet in the wake of the asset purchase program (QE) will take a while—the Federal Reserve admits as much. And what will happen if there is a recession between now and then, so that the Fed must respond again? (That question will be tackled later.)

This crucial recognition that the global economy—what we knew for decades as "normal"—has fundamentally changed constitutes our first step toward understanding the economy post-Financial Crisis. "Normal"—the late 20th and early 21st century global economic story—will probably be remembered as the golden years of growth—not dissimilar to the 1920s. In the "normal" era, understanding and responding to US monetary policy mostly depended on predicting movements in the federal funds rate. There was no need to predict whether the Fed was going to increase or decrease its asset purchases, by how much, and when. It was a simpler, more sanguine time—at least for the most part.

What many tend to forget are the policy miscalculations and missteps that exacerbated global imbalances in that era. Some of those imbalances created issues that surfaced only when the Financial Crisis hit. For example, China's current pivot toward a consumer-driven economy was, in part, necessitated by the drastic acceleration of its infrastructure investment during the Financial Crisis to stave off a crisis. The emerging commodity-producing economies benefited wildly from China's binge. In Europe, public and private debt piled up as the gulf between northern and southern countries widened and bond yields began to surge. Meanwhile, the US housing bubble kept the world's largest economy buoyant. Those were the last of the golden years.

Things are different now. It is time to understand what the world economy will be like *after normal*—that is, *after* China's infrastructure binge, *after* the US consumers' bad behavior, and *after* emerging economies' easy growth. What does the global economy look like *after* everything has changed?

AFTER (NORMAL) DEMOCRACY

Democracy Falls First?

The degradation of liberal democracy in Greece was not as immediately apparent as other fallout from the Great Recession was. Politics move slowly. Financial markets are a swift and relentless master. Democracy will survive. But how it will evolve *after normal* is a frightening question.

What happened in Greece—an unsustainable debt burden turned political crisis—can happen almost anywhere. Take, for example, a fiscally responsible nation like Ireland. When the Great Recession struck, the government of Ireland did not appear likely to succumb to a financial crisis. Then it was forced to step in to save the country's banking system, and government debt soared. Ireland has mostly recovered, but the outcome could have been much worse. Still, the point is valid: Even a fiscally responsible government can find itself caught in a terrifying scenario—and quickly. Because financial markets move far more quickly than governments do, a precipitous downturn often catches policy makers by surprise.

When governments run into financial crises, outcomes are messy. This has been true across Southern Europe to varying degrees since 2008. But Greece in particular has found itself trapped in a crucible of debt, with democracy itself at stake.

1

Generally lost in discussion of the European debt crisis has been the threat what the response to the crisis poses to the health of a liberal democracy. The debt loads of the European South precipitated not only fiscal crises across the region but democratic ones as well.

The Hellenic Republic now has more debt than it can ever repay in full—even given more bailouts and much more time. It is worthwhile to review how we got here. The 2008 Financial Crisis exposed the Greek debt problem. Government debt yields spiked. And in an effort to maintain European Union (EU) stability, the troika—the International Monetary Fund (IMF), the European Commission, and the European Central Bank (ECB)—bailed out the Greek government. This tactic kept Greece in the EU and the EU itself stable. But the troika required adjustments to the Greek economy in return for its money. The "austerity" it imposed thrust the Greek economy into a deep depression—a tunnel with no light at the end.

Greece is no longer ruled by popular vote and legislative rulemaking but instead by an unelected troika and a government with little ability to govern in the people's interest. Granted, years of irresponsible governance brought on this situation. But now the most disturbing issues on the table are the condition, functionality, and even the legitimacy of democracy in Greece. The legitimacy of democratic rule and of individual rights (such as the right to own property) is critical to the repayment of debts—and ultimately to avoiding a failed state and dictatorship. Now, though, a new, different, and unfortunate kind of democracy is in its infancy: the debt democracy.

Democracy—specifically the brand based on a durable constitution—divides power among many constituencies. This division creates a system in which it is difficult to consolidate power in the hands of a single executive. One consequence of the Greek debt crisis is the complete removal of public choice in government affairs and the ceding of power to outside interests who would impose "austerity." Greece's creditors have simply bypassed the natural dynamics of democracy in favor of imposing budgetary discipline on an irresponsible sovereign. And they did this while paying little if any attention to the long-term effects of austerity on the liberal-democratic process. Austerity in and of itself is not necessarily a bad thing. But the way the decision was made to impose it does matter. And Greece is the best example of how *not* to go about that process.

In a debt democracy, the concentration of power lies not with an elected leader but with an extranational or nongovernmental entity with the de facto power to impose its will on the debtor. Unelected outsiders control the domestic decision mechanism—and the money. The sovereignty of the nation and its citizenry is replaced by the power of the outside few, whose motives may be more pecuniary than civic.

Policies adopted under the aegis of fiscal consolidation can result in an inability to govern effectively. And demands of creditors to reduce government deficits and employment may drastically reduce the citizenry's sense of political involvement. In Greece, the people and their elected representatives do not have control over the decision-making process; the troika does. Prime Minister Tsipras made a show of standing up for his country and the interests of his people. He never stood a chance. Instead, the "strong men" of the troika made an example out of Greece.

Greece should not overlook the broader impact of delayed or too-frequent elections, the imposition and retention of a technocratic government, mandatory job and pension cuts, and a convoluted and punitive taxation system. A basic tenet of a liberal society is the rule of law. The breakdown and renegotiation of implied constitutional contracts between the people and their government undermines this tenet. A debt democracy struggles not only to keep its domestic policy apparatus from crumbling but also to maintain its legitimacy.

Crises and the dramatic, forceful changes that accompany them constitute a recipe for political turmoil. Freedom and democracy itself cannot be sacrificed to the goal of repaying debts at all costs. The most common way to measure the outcomes of austerity and restructuring programs is the interest rate on debt issued to the public. But this approach is much too narrow when the price of placating investors is the suspension or dissolution of liberal governance itself.

A debt democracy searches for a new way to rule, to overthrow its tyrannical occupiers (so to speak). The election of Syriza was a protest against the strain of living in a debt democracy. The temptation in such a crisis is to elect a powerful, nationalistic executive. Electing a leader with the will to implement internal change and provide strong leadership is not a concern in and of itself. But a problem arises when the leader exercises power in the name of reform but then establishes a dominant position in the executive branch. And to a degree this is what Greece's governing party Syriza did, not for themselves but, ironically, for the sake of the troika.

The Greek people never elected the troika, and after the bailout, the troika paid little attention to the long-term effects of its austerity policies on the liberal-democratic process. The austerity it imposed broke down the traditional democratic links, substituting a hollowed out, largely undemocratic debt democracy. At its extremes, then, excessive debt hobbles the ability of governments to act as arbiters for their citizens. Risks include not only sovereign-debt crises but also rising disenchantment with liberal democracy itself.

All Safety Nets Are Gone

Eventually, the Greek crisis will play itself out, but the process will take time. It will also have ramifications. The process of the bailout negotiations wears thin. And donors' appetites for continued bailouts dwindle. In the end, Greece cannot survive without significant concessions from creditors. Greece has been willing to undergo the austerity measures required to satisfy its creditors. Neither side wants to maintain the status quo.

While creditors are understandably weary of extending bailout after bailout, there are also institutions that risked their credibility in the process of trying to save Greece. At the center of the game was the European Central Bank. The ECB provided emergency liquidity assistance (ELA) funds to maintain liquidity at banks in Greece. If it had withheld these funds, the ECB itself would have been the primary source of volatility and instability. Thus the ECB was not only politicized, but weaponized. It made clear that it was more than capable of destroying an entire economy if its demands (in other words, Germany's demands) were not met.

The ECB had complete control over emergency funds to the Greek central bank. Greece could not be forced to leave the EU; it would have to leave voluntarily. But the ECB could have effectively forced Greece to leave by cutting the Greek banks off from ELA funding. In the midst of the crisis, cutting the banks off from their sole sourcing of funding would have forced them to close and collapse. The ECB would have set a dangerous precedent. Of course, the threat of being cut off from ECB lifelines deterred Greek officials from pushing the limits of their deals, but the Greeks ceased to view the ECB as a central bank.

The carnage would have been all too real. For Greece, exiting the euro and returning to the drachma would require the banking system to overhaul deposits and print an entirely new currency. The drachma would plummet against both the euro and the dollar. Greece's exports would be far more competitive, but Greece imports more than it exports. So Greece would almost certainly be accepting hyperinflation and a further decline in its economic output by leaving the EU and defaulting on its debt. This was not lost on Greek politicians.

The ECB was risking the confidence of other member states too, and caused them to second-guess their own willingness to be subjected to the whims of a central bank not under their own control. When the ECB acts poorly, fallout spills into investment markets as well. Investors like to have confidence that there is a backstop. The Fed during the Great Recession is an example. Fear (or worse, knowing) that a real safety net does not exist would impair confidence. But confidence is a precondition for growth. Fundamentally, central banks are the lenders of last resort, not hall monitors.

The ECB's quantitative easing relieved fears that could otherwise have spread to other peripheral or other highly indebted nations. But a crisis of confidence in the ECB's fidelity would dampen its monetary policy effectiveness. The Greek issues surrounding the ECB threatened confidence in the euro currency. The EU hardly averted a crisis of confidence in its relevancy—and shoring up confidence started with the ECB.

And then Brexit happened. Not because of the Greece or ECB—the UK always remained on the British pound—but due to the feeling of political alienation by the people of the UK. The economics of Brexit make no sense. The dissatisfaction with the EU was strong enough to brush those worries aside. The problem was not too little self-rule but too much remote rule.

Creditors and Credibility

Will the Greek drama eventually be resolved? Or will Greece continue to teeter on the precipice of default? Regardless of how the Greeks vote between now and the end of its debt woes, the ultimate outcome is someone else's decision. And here is the problem with "after normal" democracy. Even if the Greek citizenry demands change, the government does not possess the authority to implement change. If there is some sort of incident—if neither side is willing to back down or compromise—the fallout will be tragic. Though the European experiment might live on, Greece would likely be its first victim. If there is a crisis, it will not spread through financial derivatives. Transmission will flow through a lack of confidence in and understanding of the actions of the ECB and the EU elite.

The ECB's "after normal" is a disturbing precedent—not just in the case of Greece, but for countries in the monetary union that will need future assistance. Italy is a country with debt problems not dissimilar in magnitude to those of Greece. It has seen its borrowing costs wax and wane as investors grasp the lack of central-bank conviction as a backstop. Confidence is the cornerstone of modern central banking. In this way markets may challenge the ECB's role as a central bank. The ECB appears to be evolving into more of a political tool and less of a central bank.

Greece could be a symptom of a greater problem for the ECB. When it temporarily withheld ELA funds from the Greek central bank, the ECB caused immediate pain on Athen's Main Street. Italy, and others, may feel as though it too is in the crosshairs someday. This is not the financial contagion of Lehman Brothers but a contagion of confidence. Without assurances surrounding their own sovereign debt obligations, other EU member states' willingness to be subject to the whims of a disinterested central bank may diminish rapidly—especially in times of crisis.

After normal, many central banks have used most or all of their ammunition to jump-start economies. The measure of confidence that they have left is fading quickly. In the most crisis impact areas, democracy is evolving into a form of creditor rule. Those entities that bailed out Greece are—for better or worse—dictating the direction of domestic Greek policy. The ECB should take care in dealing with its member states, not because they deserve less austerity but because the ECB runs a substantial risk of destroying the only thing it has left: its credibility.

7

Rum at Risk

The US has its own turn to test its skills at avoiding a debt democracy outcome as Puerto Rico works its way through default. Puerto Rico has been in a recession for a decade with little sign of emergence. Chronic budget deficits, a bloated public sector, an economy in shambles, and highly tax-advantaged bonds that encouraged investors to stay too long should have acted as warning signs to observers, investors, and policy makers.

The island's population has declined after peaking in 2004. A tangible figure of the government bloat is that, before the crisis, nearly a quarter of all people employed on the island worked for state or local government. Gross domestic product (GDP) has followed the population and the labor force lower, exacerbating the debt-to-GDP ratio in the process.

Some of these issues stem from mainland US policies that, when combined with local island economics, create disincentives. A prime example is the interaction between the minimum wage and welfare benefits. According to research conducted by Krueger, Teja, and Wolfe, a swollen welfare benefit discourages the island's citizens from finding work. Further, 28% of hourly workers in Puerto Rico earn less than $8.50 per hour. (In the United States, the figure is about 2%.) That means they earn a paycheck of less than the welfare benefit of over $1,700.

These dynamics have driven the labor-force participation rate down to the low 40% range. When we consider the participation rate combined with the population decline, it is very difficult to imagine how the Puerto Rican workforce will return to pre-recession levels. Even then, the participation rate was less than 50%.

Policies that make sense for the US mainland economy should not automatically be imposed on Puerto Rico. Puerto Rico is a tropical island with no exploitable natural resources. The United States has a low-cost advantage in electricity pricing and low fixed costs of manufacturing. But Puerto Rico relies on oil to generate its electricity. This makes its energy expensive and inefficient.

Until recently, territories received tax advantages for economic-development purposes. The idea was to "assist the US possessions in obtaining employment-producing investments by US corporations." After 2005, IRS section 936 was no longer available to corporations, and the tax benefits to US mainland firms—particularly pharmaceutical companies—evaporated.

There was a significant amount of skepticism as to whether 936 was useful in developing the economy of Puerto Rico—or was simply a way to lower corporate tax bills. It may be coincidental, but the current recession began when the tax advantages ended.

But by no means were US mainland policies and the end of 936 solely responsible for Puerto Rico's debt accumulation. Puerto Rico overspent and diluted the urgency of the situation by making budget predictions that had no basis in reality—not to mention that its financial reporting is not timely enough to catch and reduce spending. Puerto Rico's debt level is over 100% of national GDP. This is unsustainable by any measure, not only because of the absolute level of the debt but also due to the shrinking taxable base.

Puerto Rico distills 70% of the rum consumed in the United States. We might surmise that both borrowers and lenders were imbibing too much of that product if they failed to foresee the island territory's default. The territory's creditors will suffer through legal challenges, but there will be assets transferred and debts repaid—at least partially and over long time horizons. The Puerto Rican economy was in decline before the Great Recession. It is going to take time to recover. In fact, the more of its assets Puerto Rico is forced to turn over to private hands, the faster it may recover. Without support—such as the return of section 936 and other pro-growth, low-opposition measures—Puerto Rico will be mired in a protracted economic downturn that could further exacerbate its debt problem.

Because Puerto Rico will (most likely) never be bailed out, market mechanisms and a form of pseudo-bankruptcy must sort out a solution. This situation is far different from the Greek experience, since—as the Commonwealth will likely be cut off from debt markets for some time—Puerto Rico explicitly lost its autonomy and governance.

Puerto Rico is now America's own little version of Greece. PROMESA—the Puerto Rico Oversight, Management, and Economic Stability Act—creates a fiscal control board, an entity not unlike the troika, to oversee the island's budget. Much like Greek people, the people of Puerto Rico are no longer in control of their destiny. The debt holders are in charge now. Granted, PROMESA is apparently well intentioned. But well intentioned does not mean well designed. The seizure of democracy, even if well intentioned, does not typically end well.

Debt democracies are of course a symptom of a much deeper phenomenon. Fiscal deficits and cheap financing have enabled much of the developed world to spend on social programs and populist policies. Debt used to finance popular programs and thwart economic crises across the past couple of decades had remained, until the recent financial crisis, mostly an afterthought. The ability to maintain low borrowing rates can be sustained for prolonged periods of time—think Japan—but it will not last forever. The West must be wary of the debt democracy— and the possible outcomes—when conducting and influencing economic policy.

BRICS BREAKING; SCALES TIPPING TOWARD THE WEST

It Didn't Matter... for a While

When Jim O'Neill christened Brazil, Russia, India, and China the "BRICs" in 2001, the growth engine of the global economy was supposedly in the process of shifting away from the West to the "new guard." The BRICs—which became the BRICS when South Africa was admitted to the bloc in 2010—were going to alter economic and geopolitical balance. Their economies, benefitting from the demand for commodities and cheap labor, formed the epicenter of a new, emerging, and global middle class. As this middle class prospered, economies grew. But now the BRICS economies are stumbling. Without a pivot back toward economic growth powered by infrastructure investment from China or (possibly) India, the future of these countries is in question. Were their economic prospects in fact just a mirage?

The Great Recession was not the end of the surge for the bloc. The BRICs quickly exited the downturn in 2008 and 2009. This was assisted by the price strength in commodities and an influx of yield-seeking dollars. Much of the trend was driven by the Federal Reserve's quantitative easing (QE) program, which kept interest rates at historically low levels. But when the Fed ceased its QE program, the now infamous "taper tantrum" of 2013 exposed some of the cracks in the vaunted economies.

For a time the natural-resource endowments of Brazil and Russia boosted their economic growth paths and their current-account balances. But countries cannot rely on commodity abundance and historically high prices forever. In the long run, countries blessed with abundant natural resources tend to develop less and grow at slower rates than those whose economic base is broader. Resource-rich developing and middle-income countries are searching for the mechanism that can spur the next decade of growth. But they may well be acting too late.

Brazil spent some $15 billion to build the infrastructure needed to host the Olympics and somewhat more than $15 billion for the World cup, according to middle-of-the-road estimates. This spending boosted GDP and likely positively masked the true condition of the underlying economy as commodities weakened. Now, corruption threatens to entrench the growth headwinds even more deeply as a corruption scandal roils its political elite.

Russia's economy is being assaulted from two sides as Western sanctions and persistently low oil prices stress a country unprepared to deal with falling energy prices. The deceleration in Russian GDP that started in 2010 has persisted. The Russian government receives about 50% of its revenues from oil and gas. Current prices dramatically alter the outlook for the country from that of 2013, when oil was higher and Russia appeared to be integrating into the Western global economy. Commodity abundance is the reason President Putin could spend $51 billion on, or around, the Sochi Olympics. But the Sochi spending was also peak-oil revenue spending, as budgets continue to tighten after the easy money evaporated. It is difficult to ignore the theme of commodities and global sporting events.

To be competitive in the 21st century, both Brazil and Russia needed to reinvest their commodity windfalls into forging competitiveness in the global economy. For the most part, they have failed to do so. While investments were made in infrastructure, the long-term usefulness of better Sochi roads can be questioned. Resort towns are pleasant but they should not be built up at the expense of the longer-term needs of national economies.

Meanwhile, India and China are struggling to pivot their economies toward more sustainable internal growth. With a relatively low debt-to-GDP ratio, India could finance vitally needed infrastructure investments. A more competent regulatory environment is pivotal for India. The recent move to ban large denomination cash bills was a direct attempt to take steps in this direction. China is attempting to transition toward a more balanced economy, shifting from an export-driven to an internal-consumption model. Even if this difficult transition is successful, though, China's long-term sustainable growth rate will fall below its level of recent decades. An aging population with a diminishing number of workers is a strong headwind against building a consumer economy. The relaxation of China's one-child policy is unlikely to be a panacea in the near term. Instead, economic growth will inevitably continue to moderate. How quickly the deceleration happens will have repercussions for the global economy—but also for internal stability.

With the exception of China, GDP growth among the BRICS is now fairly mundane. And this trajectory will continue. There are few if any catalysts at hand for energizing growth with exception pf India. The BRICS must be conscious of the middle income trap, especially where wages are rising, cost competitiveness is beginning to decline, and advanced industry and technology have yet to take root.

But the BRICS should be even more conscious of the possibility that their middle classes may lose ground. The "emerging middle class" was one of the great stories of the opening of the 21st century. The next decade may see the storyline pivot to the stagnation or erosion of the middle class, much as we see unfolding in the US. The next crisis may well come from the BRICS as they fight for economic growth in a world where growth is hard to come by. They are certain to fail in being the growth drivers they once were.

In light of the slowdown in the BRICS, the United States does not look like such a laggard. The West has been a persistent drag on the global economy's fitful return to growth after the Financial Crisis. But now the West is rebounding, and its economic importance is waxing, not waning. The next leg of growth that the BRICs are searching for lies a long way off. Yet, even as the BRICs struggle, the global economy is poised to benefit from growth, however modest, from the West.

And Trade May Only Hasten the Decline

Marginal optimism in the West's ability to grow is rooted in its ability to rely on internal, rather than predominantly external, demand. The Transatlantic Trade and Investment Partnership (TTIP) could be critically important for the future trajectory of both the US and EU economies. Already critical markets for one another, the EU and US trade relationship accounts for about 30% of global trade. This relationship may become much cozier soon, to the detriment of the emerging world.

Normally, free trade agreements (FTAs) break down barriers to trade by lowering and removing tariffs. But tariffs are already low between the world's two largest economies. Lowering non-tariff barriers to trade would remove a number of underlying impediments to trade between the US and EU. These include everything from technical requirements on goods to health and agricultural standards. For the TTIP to have a pronounced economic impact, regulatory standards will need to be integrated significantly. Mutual recognition of standards—the EU's recognizing the FDA's standards of approval in drug development, for example—could benefit both economies. With the US and EU together constituting about 50% of the world's economy, setting firm, mutually recognized standards could spur a de facto global standards regime.

The TTIP is a chance for the US and EU to not only compete more favorably with the emerging world but to spur growth in a time of potential stagnation on both sides of the Atlantic. The Organisation for Economic Co-operation and Development (OECD) estimated that the TTIP could boost the EU economy by 3%–3.5%. More than a million jobs could be created in the US. Spain and Italy could see 140,000. The UK more than 400,000. And per capita income could rise more than 6% in Spain, 10% in the UK, and 13% in the US. These are not trivial gains.

Not everyone should be thrilled. A successfully implemented TTIP would erode the value of trade agreements already in place. Some countries that have long been trade partners with the US and EU will suffer. The US' North American Free Trade Agreement (NAFTA) neighbors, Mexico and Canada, will suffer relative trade losses as their trade treatment loses its exclusivity. In this case, the renegotiation by the Trump Administration might not be the greatest headwind to Mexico and Canada. This likely explains the push by Mexico's then ambassador to the United States, Eduardo Medina Mora, for Mexico's inclusion in the TTIP. The BRICS will find their longstanding advantages of low-cost labor and production slipping. BRICS' trade losses to the US and EU could, according to estimates from the Bertelsmann Foundation, amount to more than 30% of export and import trade. At a time when the steep drop-off in commodities sales is already ravaging their economies, this deep loss could be a final straw.

However, the success of the TTIP is not guaranteed. France has little to gain from it and therefore little incentive to bargain. It has already managed to eliminate "cultural exceptions" from the negotiations. Germany and the UK have the most to gain from the TTIP. With the UK no longer part of the negotiation, it removes a motivated participant. They were looking for the most comprehensive TTIP possible. The TTIP was, in fact, one reason for the UK to remain in the EU. Now, it must negotiate a separate trade agreement with the US.

The TTIP is not a silver bullet, and its potential economic benefits should be met with at least some skepticism. The predicted gains are too good to be true. If the US were to gain the entirety of its 1.1 million potential jobs, that number would be roughly equivalent to five months' worth of jobs gains in a healthy economy. There is little question that a well implemented TTIP tips the global playing field once more in favor of the developed world.

While politically difficult to enact, its ultimate outcome has significant ramifications for the future of global trade and regulatory standards. The economic benefits sorely sought by both sides of the Atlantic outweigh some of the differences in regulatory thought. With the prospect for meaningful GDP and job gains in the US, maybe the TTIP is the push the US economy needs to maintain the current recovery. It might also be a means for the EU to begin to reduce unemployment and accelerate growth. However, the Trump Administration has expressed skepticism in gains from trade. The TTIP is therefore far from certain to be ratified.

For the West to regain its place of leadership and prominence in the global economy, there must be some leadership shown. The TTIP is a way for the US and EU to reassert their global economic importance and to boost domestic growth in the medium term. At the same time, TTIP poses a substantial threat to the already fragile economies of the BRICS.

But Would the TPP Have Saved Asia?

Probably not. The Trans-Pacific Partnership (TPP) would have boosted some Asian countries through trade with the US. But China, the country whose economic success largely determines the fate of the rest of the region, was never party to the agreement. The now dead TPP could have been economically transformative—just not for the US or China.

The American goal for TPP was never centered on economic benefit. Instead, it was targeted toward engaging with emerging Asia and being present while the new rules of global trade are being set. Exports and privileged access to the US market benefit emerging Asia. The US and Japan could also act as an economic counterbalance to China in the region, helping the smaller, less-developed countries compete for export growth.

Developed countries such as the US, Canada, and Australia were set to gain little economically from the TPP, because these nations already have trade agreements in place. The US has long since ratified NAFTA with Mexico and Canada and has deals on the books with Peru, Singapore, Australia, and Chile as well. Estimates by Petri, Plummer, and Zhai place US GDP gains from TPP at only 0.13%, or $27 billion, by 2025.

The US was too big to benefit from the deal. And many of the other nations involved were already tied together through other agreements. Even if the entirety of the $210 billion annual benefit to global GDP from TPP were to accrue solely to the US in 2025, that amount would have only added about 1% to GDP.

One, now shattered, breakthrough would have been an FTA between the US and Japan. To an extent, the lack of cooperation in trade between these two countries has benefited the US. Japanese auto companies, for instance, have moved production to facilities in Kentucky and elsewhere in the US. Japan has also been hesitant to enter an FTA with the US because of the sensitivity surrounding its agriculture industry, though this concern appears to have been assuaged, if not overcome. Even with the failure of TPP, there may be room for the US and Japan to come to the table on trade.

Services should be the area where the US is predominantly focused in trade negotiations going forward. This is where the

US excels. The US consistently runs a trade surplus in services—in 2016 this figure was $248 billion. Around 90% of private US employment is in services or service-focused industries. The sector embodies the lion's share of US competitiveness today and should continue to be a considerable strength going forward.

When the US negotiated TPP, the focus was clearly not the US economy. Its death was more tragic for Southeast Asia than for the US. The potential gains from the passage of a strong TTIP far outweigh those from the TPP. The benefits of the TPP were expected to come down the road as more countries join the framework and trade became increasingly liberalized. With the TPP killed and the TTIP seemingly on life-support, the gains from trade are unlikely to be realized in the near-term.

With so little to gain in terms of economic growth, the US was gambling that it could play a more substantial role in future trade negotiations and participate in setting policies. If large Asian trading partners were to join, for example, their involvement could increase the partnership's cache, contribute more economic growth, and so on. But this scenario was unlikely to happen in the near term. Instead, the TPP was an investment in the long-term liberalization of trade.

Without China and the BRICS, Where Will the Global Economy End Up?

As the US attempted to partner with its neighbors and construct trade systems and norms, China's GDP growth was beginning to decelerate. The days of 10% growth are over. Despite the slowdown, however, China should continue to contribute more than any other country to global growth.

Why is China's growth rate gearing down? In part, Chinese demographics have contributed to the country's success. With 1.3 billion people, China is the most populous country on the planet. Its economy has benefitted from a tremendous inflow of people from the countryside to the cities. Though more migration to cities is expected, China's aging population is shrinking the working-age population. And rising costs for the care of the elderly constitute strong economic headwinds. Demographics inexorably impact economies, though changes evolve slowly enough for the next growth engine to emerge (if there's one to be had).

Which countries and regions may one day replace Chinese growth? Russia, India, and Brazil have not yet had their moment. Russia, at 2–3% growth, has yet to live up to its hype. India, on the other hand, boasts the world's youngest and second-largest population. India's contribution to global growth is projected to grow to around 10% by the end of the decade. Brazil is perpetually plagued by its reliance on commodity prices, which are inevitably subject to boom and bust cycles. It contributes only 3%–4% to global growth in good times. In fact, Russia, India, and Brazil supply surprisingly little to overall global growth—especially since the commodity bubble has burst. The RIBs have little meat on their bones.

At least for now, then, there is no other "China" poised to emerge as the next engine of global growth. For now, the US and China are the dominant forces of global growth, combining for around 50%. There will come a time when the global economy needs the next China. For a global economy awash in excess capacity, the dearth of promising candidates looks particularly distressing.

How Will Asian Powers React to the Shifting China?

Australia and China boomed hand in hand. Australian resources fueled Chinese infrastructure investment. And Australia built out its own infrastructure to deal with Chinese demand. But this story of mutual growth may be ending. China's infrastructure boom is at best slowing and at worst ending.

The fact that Australian exports are predominantly commodities leaves Australia in a difficult economic position. In 2016, China consumed more than 28% of Australia's exports, an extreme concentration. Japan, the second-most-popular destination for Australian exports, consumed slightly less than 12%, and third-place US took 7%, according to the Australian Bureau of Statistics. Australia has not yet forged the same ties to India that it has to China. In fact, exports to India have fallen by a quarter since the middle of 2010. This has in part been due to a decline in the value of gold exports.

At the start of the 21st century, trade between China and Australia amounted to around 7 billion Aussie dollars annually. Since then, it has exploded by more than 1200%—to $93 billion Aussie dollars in 2016. This A$86 billion increase constitutes almost half the A$185 billion total gain in exports that Australia has made so far this century. Politically, however, the relationship between Australia and China is not always amicable. The Australian government, citing national security concerns, barred the Chinese technology company Huawei from bidding on the Australian National Broadband Network project. At the time, the largest infrastructure project to be undertaken in Australia's history.

Despite their periodic differences, Australia and China have become deeply intertwined economically. But it may be time for Australia to begin planning its next move, as China slows its infrastructure investments. Australia, in other words, needs another infrastructure boom. And so does India. India's 12th Five-Year Plan suggested that about $1 trillion should be spent on infrastructure over the 2012–2017 timeframe. This would equate to 10% of GDP every year being spent on infrastructure. And geographically speaking, Australia would be ideally situated to take advantage of an Indian infrastructure boom. Much-needed infrastructure investments would deliver a necessary boost to economic growth for India. And India could be a new mega-customer for Australia that would mitigate the economic impact of China's weakening growth. None of these goals were accomplished, leaving much of the work still to be done.

Any infrastructure boom would not be seamless though. The funding for the infrastructure may not be easy to come by in India's poor capital markets. At one point, China offered to finance $300 billion of the spending. But given the history of border disputes between China and India, this gesture was seen more as political posturing than a potential investment. India should be tempted by the funding, though. India needs infrastructure, a reality highlighted by the blackout that left more than 650 million people without power in the summer of 2012. Investment in the electric grid is critical to economic growth. Roads and bridges matter too. The problems created by India's infrastructure deficits can be fixed only slowly and at great cost. In 2010, McKinsey estimated the cost to be about $45 billion per year. An investment in infrastructure would boost the Indian economy with employment gains from the construction itself. And it would have the long-term benefit of reducing a bottleneck in the Indian economy.

Unfortunately for India and Australia, correcting the infrastructure deficit is not a simple task. The Chinese commitment had the potential to bring other global players to the table, but red tape and financing are significant headwinds. Not to mention the historical political tensions. Indian Prime Minister Modi should have moved quickly on the economic plan his party has proposed. The Bharatiya Janata Party's (BJP) election manifesto called for building 100 new cities "adhering to concepts like sustainability, walk to work, etc." The plan was ambitiously unaccomplished. Many of the ideas make economic sense. Incubators designed to nurture start-ups and provide support for entrepreneurs and improving the lives of women are examples. But accomplishing all of the goals in the medium or even long term will be nearly impossible.

The BJP manifesto offered a long-term road map of what India needs to be successful, even though the notion of building 100 new cities may sound excessive, bringing to mind the ghost cities of China. However, India will require new cities to accommodate continuing urbanization. McKinsey estimates that India's cities will be home to 11% of the global urban population by 2025. As people migrate from rural to urban areas, wages and spending tend to increase. Trailing China in urbanization and with a population of more than 1.2 billion people, India has ample room to begin the shift from the farm to the city. India is both more populous and less urbanized than China is. If the BJP plan is eventually implemented—even marginally—the benefits to Australia could be similar in many respects to those from the Chinese boom.

There is some movement between Australia and India to deepen ties. The Australia-India Comprehensive Economic Cooperation Agreement is in its ninth round of negotiations, and there appears to be support for the agreement in Australia. A study finds that while the agreement would benefit Australia more than it would India, it would still help both. At the moment, however, the level of Australian exports to India tends to be volatile and heavily tied to commodity prices.

Australia cannot turn its back on China either. China and Australia were in talks for a free-trade agreement of their own for about a decade. China is likely to slow its growth in infrastructure spending in coming years. Still, estimates suggest that China, ghost cities and all, will see 13 million people per year move to cities between now and 2030—more than the population of New York City every 12 months. Thus the level of China's infrastructure spending is unlikely to drop markedly over the medium term.

Are these existing and potential collaborations the first signs of an Asian economic trio? Possibly, but it will take a tremendous amount of cooperation between countries that historically have not been overly friendly. China is scouring the world for investment options. India can oblige, and Australia can supply the material. Australia, though shifting from an overly heavy reliance on China, would be more tied to China than ever before in other ways. For all three countries to reach their full potential, they must cooperate. Australia has yet to reap the full benefit from one of the great urbanization stories of the 21st century. India's expected tempered rate of urbanization would be better for Australia than the Chinese boom has been. A steady, slow, and long urbanization cycle in India would allow Australia to maintain its economic strength while avoiding internal economic bubbles. There will still be volatility, however. With the concentration of trade to China, there can be little else, and the need to find their *after normal* trading partner to pick up the slack is critical.

The US Is Not the Only Trading Partner Anymore

We have reached a critical juncture for the future of free trade and America's role in shaping it. But the United States is stepping away—or at the least threatening to step away—from the global economy at precisely the incorrect moment. A retreat from global trade, accompanied by threats of sanctions and fines, would do far more damage to the image and trustworthiness of America than anything else. With US legitimacy and stability in question, China and others may be seen as viable alternatives to a tumultuous United States. The simple truth of global trade is that the United States is not the only game in town.

As the third largest economy in the world on the nominal GDP basis (it is the largest by some measures), other nations already have plenty of incentive to engage in trade negotiations with China. The Chinese, in support of their "One Belt, One Road" initiative, have begun to build institutions similar to Western ones to encourage trade and investment.

Granted, the US remains the dominant economy. But others are catching up and becoming increasingly important to the growth of the global economy. China and India contribute more to global growth than does the West. The US and EU together are optimistically 25% of global economic growth. But China and India will contribute closer to 45%. Access to a combination of China and India could soon be more tempting than access to a politically volatile United States.

One of the largest and most reviled, potential US trade agreements was the Trans-Pacific Partnership. It was one of the first sacrifices to the after normal fair trade forces. For the United States, the TPP was less about growing the US economy and more about increasing its relevance in Asia. The TPP would have been one of the largest trade deals ever, with about 40% of global GDP participating. However, the deal faced opposition from both sides of the US political chasm. To a certain degree, political rhetoric in an election year was to be expected, but the follow-through was swift. At current rhetorical levels, the passage of any meaningful trade agreement seems increasingly unlikely regardless of the potential benefits.

Meanwhile, prospects for the TTIP—the free trade deal between the US and EU—are increasingly dim. The deal could have strengthened the economies of the Western world, providing a much-needed economic boost in a time of stagnation. But there is increasing skepticism from both sides about the deal. With substantial trade between the United States and EU already in place, nontariff barriers—such as regulations and legal barriers—are being discussed for possible elimination. Breaking down these barriers is important to produce trade gains. But they also tend to be very controversial.

For the United States, the failure of these agreements, or legislator's failure to move them forward, would squelch trade negotiations for the foreseeable future. Few countries or trading blocs would want to exert the political energy and resources to tackle a trade agreement with a country that may not consummate the relationship.

The retreat from the TPP and TTIP could spur a rash of new deals between other nations. It is only natural that jilted participants will search elsewhere for growth. And it will not be difficult to find it.

In Asia, the US-led TPP deal was probably always second best to the Regional Comprehensive Economic Partnership (RCEP). The RCEP is a stunning undertaking. Not only is it outside of the sphere of US influence, but it includes China, India, South Korea, ASEAN, Australia, and New Zealand. In terms of global growth, the RCEP is the center of it.

Following a disintegration of the TPP, participants will turn to the RCEP and look to gain access to China and India—neither of whom is included in the TPP. For Mexico and Canada, who have access to the United States through the NAFTA (at least for now), this could be the preferred outcome.

Greece already has plans to apply for membership in the Asian Infrastructure Investment Bank, arguably the first of many collisions between the newly created Eastern institutions and the half-century-old Western institutions. The West's—or at least the US'—skepticism toward free trade may accelerate the trend.

According to an early 2017 Pew Research Center poll, Americans support free trade agreements by a narrow margin of 44% to 38%. Strikingly, democrats and those who lean democrat are more likely to support free trade agreements. The poll showed 67% of democrats say free trade agreements have been a good thing for the US. Only 36% of republicans say the same. Certainly, there are downsides to free trade, but it would be a mistake for the United States to abandon it. China and its growing sphere of institutions are viable options in case the United States drops the ball. The US is not the only trade game in town.

Why the Middle Class Is Dying

Not too long ago, the US economy could carry the world. But now the US finds itself in a precarious position. The skills gap is widening, the middle class is shrinking, and wages are stagnant. America has overinvested in short-term fixes that mask the underlying issues. But it has underinvested in areas of competitiveness over the past several decades. Ostensibly a response to labor-market shocks brought on by recessions, the low interest rates of the early 2000s and the experimentation with multiple QE programs are, on a deeper level, attempts to compensate for titanic shifts in the labor market.

Long ago, the US began to lose much of its low-end manufacturing overseas. More recently, automation has had a pronounced effect. In terms of overall impact, manufacturing peaked at 22% of payrolls in 1977 and is under 9% today. A recent uptick would seem to be a positive and well reported piece of news for the US economy. But the new manufacturing is not labor intensive and creates few jobs relative to what left. Many of the returning or newly created manufacturing jobs require the ability to operate and program complex machinery. The dismal US education system does not prepare students for these realities. Americans have skills, but the skills and talents do not seem to match current employer needs.

Far more troubling, though, is the loss of employment in occupations once considered safe from offshoring and technological advances. It is not just manufacturing that can be outsourced and mechanized anymore. The ceaseless march of technology and increasing speed of internet connectivity are constantly creating and recreating an entirely new competitive landscape—this time for service jobs. The new global class of cheap-but-educated labor is alien to anything the US worker has ever experienced. Today, a routine or repetitive knowledge job can be moved to the developing world or replaced altogether with computing power.

The result is that well-paying service jobs are leaving the US—or are simply never being created here. Instead, new customer service centers are built in India, and robots are the first to be hired. Any job a robot can do or that a computer program can automate is under siege.

Alan Blinder estimates 22% to 29% of US jobs can potentially be moved offshore. Not all will move, but all are contestable. What is a "contestable job"? One that might not necessarily be outsourced but one that is now exposed to international competition. This global competition limits wage pressures businesses feel in certain areas of employment. If a job is contestable on an international scale, a US worker is competing with cheap talent around the world—not just in the next cubicle. This limits a workers ability to negotiate wages. Negotiate too much, and the robot or foreign call center begins to look a lot better to management. As breakthroughs in information technology cause the number of globally contestable jobs to increase, the global flattening of wages across tradable services industries is likely to continue.

According to the Census Bureau, median household income peaked in 1999 and has steadily declined with only a slight reprieve before the housing bubble burst. Adjusted for inflation, the 2015 US median income was below the 1999 level. The step-up in competition for middle class jobs from developing nations is, essentially, a step down (or at best sideways) for US middle class, middle wage job prospects.

With few good jobs left and fewer being created, middle income wages have stagnated. According to Goldman Sachs, there were relatively few lost jobs on the high and low end of the wage spectrum during the Financial Crisis, and these jobs bounced back quickly. The middle suffered much greater losses, and their recovery has been slower. It is a middle class rout, and perhaps only the middle class itself appreciates what is happening.

A 2012 Pew Research Center report, aptly subtitled "Fewer, Poorer, Gloomier," showed an American middle class that is less optimistic. 26% thought the next generation's standard of living would be worse than theirs. Between 1971 and 2011, Pew estimated the proportion of middle class households declined from 61% to 51%, and their share of total income declined from 62% in 1970 to 45% in 2010.

The impact of the middle classes malaise will not be restricted to the middle class itself. There will be spillover effects. The shrinking of the middle class and stagnant wage growth are disinflationary forces. With wages flat, the middle class cannot increase consumption and pay more for housing. Much of this is apparent already as the US economy struggles to grow demand.

Highly skilled services and manufacturing are areas where the US currently maintains a comparative advantage. Typically, high wage occupations benefit from tradability. Creative, education-intensive industries are not being offshored or replaced with technology—at least not yet. At the moment, these are the jobs the US has an advantage in producing and exporting. These are uncontestable jobs. Technological improvements tend to enhance these jobs, not replace them. But there are no guarantees. The new reality demands being brilliant or different. Mundane will not cut it.

The US needs to protect its comparative advantage in services. Losing this, now or in the future, could be catastrophic. A consistent decline in educational outcomes indicates the US may not be setting itself up well for future competition. Mediocre PISA test scores are one thing, but the fact that US students did poorly at creative problem solving is a red flag.

This is the middle skills gap. Skilled services that guaranteed middle class status a generation ago are no longer produced in the US. And the US continues to prepare a workforce for an economy that no longer exists. Currently, the US has a comparative advantage in high-end services, which produces a trade surplus and jobs growth. But the US is currently blind to a titanic shift in its competitive advantages in the coming decades. The US must shift its focus toward developing employees with the skills to bypass the middle skill gap. Highly skilled tradable sectors should be nurtured and encouraged. Ignoring them will consign the middle class to a continued skills gap and economic stagnation.

But the US Has a Dynamic Economy

Where are all the jobs? Conventional wisdom holds that small businesses are the engine of employment growth, a possible solution to a perceived lack of labor-market dynamism.

And small businesses are critical to a healthy US economy: 97% of all firms have less than 100 employees. But it is startups, which just happen to be among the smallest firms, that drive employment growth. Between 1994 and 2000—the first golden years of tech, these newly born businesses contributed an average of 190% of newly created jobs. Put another way, startups created jobs and older firms destroyed them. Startups were creating jobs even in the middle of the Great Recession. Granted, the job creation slowed, but it never dried up.

The question economists should be asking is whether entrepreneurs are creating a sufficient number of new companies. And more to the point, whether these companies are creating the needed jobs.

According to the Bureau of Labor Statistics (BLS), startups are being born at about the same rate as before the recession. The number of business births, after rising throughout the '90s and the early '00s, declined as the Great Recession took hold. But the bounce back was rapid. Business births have averaged 219,000 since the beginning of 2010 through the later part of 2016—more than the 2002 to 2007 average of 208,000.

The problem is that the number of jobs an average startup brings into this world (i.e., birth weight) has been in steady decline. During the '90s, newly birthed businesses came with six new jobs. By 2007, they came with four. And this "small baby" phenomenon will continue.

There remains a particular entrepreneurial vibrance in the US economy. People are starting companies at the same rate as before the recession. But steadily fewer people are tied to each new business. This is a function of the increase in US labor productivity. In the third quarter of 1998, the US economy brought 200,000 new businesses and 1.2 million new jobs into the world. When the same number of establishment births occurred in the fourth quarter of 2010, there were only 787,000 jobs associated with them—a 37% decline.

Births, and in general young firms (open for less than one year), are by far the most critical component of employment growth. Startups create jobs and older firms destroy them. But the past decade has seen a slow and steady decline in the number of jobs they contribute. Between March 1999 and March 2000, young firms created 4.6 million net jobs. During the same period in 2012 to 2013, there were 2.8 million created by young firms. This was still well above the total 2.55 million jobs created—but not enough. Old businesses were a drag on employment growth in both periods, accentuating the importance of young firms in creating jobs.

And young businesses fail at an extremely high rate. For example, of the 634,000 businesses born between March 1999 and March 2000, only 212,000 were still around by March 2010—a 66% fail rate. Most jobs are created in the US economy by startups, but most people work for older firms. Older firms don't create jobs, they preserve—and eventually destroy—them.

The entrepreneurial spirit of the US economy is intact. There are still enticements to start businesses, create new products, and innovate. It is the dynamism of the labor market that has declined as the efficiency of startups has increased. Startups are launching with fewer employees and not accelerating their hiring quickly even if they survive. The average number of employees for a middle-aged firm (five years old) is around eight.

Young companies delivered more than four million new jobs to the US economy a decade ago. But advances in technology have increased efficiency and slashed the necessary labor. This trend is not going to reverse itself. Efficiency is unlikely to decline. The obvious solution is to encourage more entrepreneurs to make up the lost jobs. To fix the problem, the US needs to encourage the startup culture. This is America's startup problem. The spirit is there, but the jobs are lacking.

I Remember When...

America has a startup problem, and the population is growing old. The boomers—the very generation that drove the US economic miracle—would now seem to be driving us off a demographic "cliff" as decades of booming consumption and labor-force growth reverse course. But this is not the entire picture. Certain trends suggest that these fears might be overstated. Instead, an entrepreneurship boom may still lie ahead of the United States.

For one thing, people are working later in life than they used to. In 1993, the labor force participation rate for people 65 and over was 11.5%. It had increased to 18.5 percent 20 years later. The BLS projects it will be 22% by 2024. Much of this gain will be driven by the increased participation of women in older age brackets, where the annual growth rate should exceed 3%. This trend should continue, and as the boomers age, they are expected to work later into life than recent generations, with 13.5% of those over 75 remaining in the labor force in 2024.

A Pew Research Center survey of people 65 and older who worked found the majority did so because they wanted to "feel useful." It also found they were more likely to enjoy their job. A full 54% compared to 29% of people 16–64. While retired from their career, boomers are likely to continue to work either simply to keep themselves busy or to supplement their retirement savings.

Conversely, fewer and fewer young people are expected to participate in the labor markets. Great educational attainment is pushing down the participation rate in the lowest age brackets. But it also increases the participation of older workers. The composition of the US labor force has shifted decisively away from manufacturing and toward services and other jobs that take less of a toll on the body, allowing employees to work for longer. Increased educational attainment leads to "greater and later" participation.

As people live and work longer, human capital continues to accumulate. There is incentive to monetize the accumulated knowledge of a career over as long time horizon as possible. We should anticipate people will work later into life as their educational attainment levels rise and their careers start later. It may be worth considering changing the definition of "working age" to encompass a more mature (on average) workforce. Another trend shows people retiring from the 9-to-5 grind but continuing to work. Often, retirement is temporary.

At this point, we may have visions of a nation of Walmart greeters, but perhaps counterintuitively, an aging workforce might help the United States maintain its entrepreneurial atmosphere and innovation advantage—more business births and, therefore, more jobs. Entrepreneurship is widely considered to be a young person's game, but this is a misconception. According to the Kauffman Firm Survey, the most entrepreneurial age bracket is between the ages of 35 and 54, or even older, and the proportion of people founding businesses over the age of 55 is greater than the 25–34-year-old crowd. One survey finds the sweet spot to be age 40, and another, 45.

Entrepreneurial activity is pivotal to the health of the US labor market and the economy in general. Remember, businesses open less than a year create the majority of jobs. This is critical to understanding why the boomers may not be done leaving their positive mark on the economy. The reason is simple: The best type of entrepreneurship—serial—increases with age. As entrepreneurial boomers head toward retirement, it is likely many of them will shift to being serially entrepreneurial or serial start-up funders.

The number of those 35–54-year-old prime candidates for entrepreneurship is actually rising and will not peak until around 2030. And while the labor force is aging, the BLS projects the median age of the workforce in 2024 will be about 42—the entrepreneurial sweet spot. The number of boomers will create problems that require solving, and they themselves are prime candidates for identifying solutions.

And even if they don't start new businesses themselves, boomer funding and mentorship could encourage a surge in the formation of startups. The boomers are the wealthiest portion of US society, and—since the housing bust destroyed one of the primary mechanisms with which 35–54-year-old entrepreneurs finance their ventures—it might be that the generational transfer of wealth is best used as a financing mechanism for startups.

There are reasons to fret, but the dynamism of the US economy is not going to fall simply because the demographics are growing older. In fact, the United States is still looking forward to its largest group of prime entrepreneurs. The boomers may yet bring the US its golden years of start-ups.

The Houseless Recovery

As previously noted, housing equity and ownership has been a key financing mechanism for startups. But housing never quite made a comeback. Select any data point except for home prices, and the tepid recovery is evident. Both single family housing starts and new one family houses sold are barely above their previous cycle lows. Home prices have risen, but this is due in part to stimulative monetary policy and the constrained housing supply toward the latter part of the current economic recovery. Housing simply did not bounce back with vigor, and it shows few signs of accelerating soon.

Every recovery is missing something. There was ample commentary about the "jobless" recoveries that began to appear in the '90s. At that time, it was fueled by job polarization (the trend toward jobs at the high end and low end of the spectrum with fewer in the middle) and increasing productivity (output per worker). The phenomenon could be due to structural shifts that antiquate certain jobs. In a 2003 speech (during a jobless recovery), soon-to-be Federal Reserve Chair Bernanke stated he favored the increase in productivity view.

The current "houseless" recovery is somewhat different. While employment now exceeds its previous highs, single-family home sales or construction are unlikely to make it back to their long-term averages in the near future. Forget surpassing the previous highs. This lack of resurgence has an effect on the broader economy. While housing itself does not constitute a significant portion of the US economy, its derivatives do. These include the non-contestable (or very low contestability) construction jobs and the boost to personal consumption—which does make up a significant portion of the economy.

What is causing the after normal economy to have a houseless recovery? For one, the homeownership rate in the US is in secular decline. This has been happening for a decade—long before the housing crisis accelerated the trend. These lower rates are especially evident in lower age groups. For those who owned homes before the financial crisis, lower levels of equity in their homes made their wealth the most susceptible to declines in prices. Much like the jobless recovery of the early 2000s, the houseless recovery's defining trend is not going to reverse quickly.

Granted, there are bright spots to a slow housing recovery. Student debt is holding back first-time buyers and will take time to pay down. This benefits multifamily housing starts, which have recovered to historical levels and are even slightly higher than the trend prior to the recession. As the home ownership rate continues to fall, sustained demand for apartments is likely to continue. This may well be a more permanent trend than many are anticipating.

Understanding the houseless recovery enlightens some of the Federal Reserve decision making. The jobless recovery of the early 2000s was at least partly responsible for the prolonged monetary accommodativeness of the Fed before the Great Recession. There is, after all, a dual mandate that calls for the Fed to maintain stable prices and maximum employment. This is arguably impossible. In the Bernanke speech referenced earlier, he stated that due to subdued inflation, the Fed could remain accommodative to support this recovery without being worried about potential negative consequences. That statement did not age well.

Does the same apply to the houseless recovery? The US has spent the last seven years attempting to reach escape velocity. Part of the reason for the struggle has been housing. In her testimony before Congress, Fed Chair Yellen admitted that lower-than-expected housing activity could be "protracted." But few are willing to admit that housing may not be coming back. Such an admission would have a considerable effect on the administration of monetary policy. It is time for the US to embrace the after normal houseless recovery.

Rental Nation

The houseless recovery is a sign of a pivot, at the very least temporarily, in the way Americans live. Homeownership has fallen below 64% to new, all-time lows. Meanwhile, vacancy rates for rental units hit lows not seen since the 1980s. In terms of employment and GDP, the economy has certainly made progress since the housing bubble burst (though both took longer to get back to normal than most expected). As noted before, housing itself, however, has continued to lag.

This shift toward rental housing has already begun to filter through one of the more important, and stagnant, parts of the economic recovery: inflation. Price moves are difficult to track. So are policies surrounding how to measure them. Some price shifts matter more than others. Oil and food movements are volatile and therefore less important than the movement of clothing and autos. The consumer price index (CPI) places significant importance on the price changes of rent and owner's equivalent rent (OER) which make up about 33% of CPI.

How much does shelter affect the CPI? Core CPI—all items less the volatile food and energy—is dominated by shelter—where rent and OER are categorized. Removing or ignoring shelter from CPI would reveal a much different—and distorted—picture. The price of shelter has consistently risen at between a 2 and 3% pace during the recovery. This is a significant reason CPI has shown any strength. This begins to make the Fed's "stable prices" mandate and self-derived 2% inflation target look suspect and less well targeted than might be assumed. This is where the shift away from ownership toward rent begins to make an impact.

The calculation of this shelter component of CPI is an oddity. The pricing data used to calculate the pricing movements is collected solely from renters—including the data used to compute the OER. The Consumer Expenditure Survey (CES) asks owners how much rent they would charge for their unfurnished home per month with no utilities. But this CES data is used only to set the weights in the CPI. Renters are asked how much their rent is per month and what amenities are included in the rent. And this is used to calculate OER—the prices used to calculate CPI are all from renters. Can you really compute rent of an owned home from a rental unit?

This means the pace of rent increases has a significant effect on the US inflation rate—not simply through the rent line but through the method of calculating OER. *Actual home prices do not enter into the equation.* If rent does not increase in concert with home prices for idiosyncratic reasons, then home price increases will not be reflected in the OER line. Again, this line is derived from information provided by renters. The converse is also true. If rents are increasing due to Millennials failing to purchase homes and instead bidding up rents, lackluster home prices will have little to no effect on the CPI.

Imagine home prices are increasing. A homeowner asked "How much would the rent on your house be?" will likely estimate a higher figure than before, due to the increasing value. While the estimation of the rent from a home owner is suspect, it may capture a bit of the underlying housing dynamic in the US. But instead, this would increase the weight of the OER in the CPI basket and have no direct bearing on the OER price level.

This may seem trivial, but there are side effects when the story begins to unwind. As (if) renters shift to being home owners, demand for rental units falls. This in turn leads to lower rents being charged to tenants. As more people own homes, the weight given to OER increases, but as rental prices decline, so does the implied rent figure. The outcome would be lower shelter inflation—while housing prices are increasing—and lower overall CPI inflation readings due to the combination of an increased weight to OER and decelerating or declining rent inflation numbers.

But who cares? The CPI is the most familiar measure of price level movements. It is used to calculate a host of things including Social Security payment increases, deflating retail sales, and the national product accounts. The measurement of CPI is critical, and this means OER is important—not simply because it makes up a significant portion of CPI but because CPI is a critical factor in other economic indicators.

There are also potential implications for Fed policy. The measurement and level of CPI is pervasive in economic indicators. The Fed's mandate is to maintain stable prices. This means the Fed needs to understand the underlying dynamics of the indicators—especially the indicators that capture headlines and affect every day economic decision making such as CPI.

The Fed would normally care little about the internals of the housing market so long as financial stability is maintained. But due to the significance of CPI, the Fed has an obligation to monitor the effects of monetary policy on shifts in housing preferences. The Fed has a habit of insisting that certain economic oddities are simply "transitory." If high levels of rent inflation are transitory, the Fed's much sought-after inflation pressures might be also.

With CPI (less shelter) already running at low levels, it is important to understand how OER will react to increasing interest rates. If interest rate increases cause rents to decline, this could be an additional headwind for inflation. Higher rates could push the United States toward deflationary territory. After all, shelter regularly contributes 50% of inflation in a given month.

Monetary policy decisions based on CPI or one of its many derivatives could be problematic. If rents begin to decline, so will inflation. Even a slowing in rent growth would be problematic for the Fed's price stability mandate. Without a more broad-based increase in the price level, the moderate rise will be difficult to maintain, and inflation will falter. Understanding this is crucial when evaluating the strength of the US recovery and the dangers posed by weak inflation.

The Fed Now Has a Millennial Problem

The Federal Reserve has waited and waited for inflation to materialize. The CPI shows prices are higher by less than 2% in 2017 than a year ago, and there are reasons to believe that this will continue. There is also a reason to be skeptical of persistent inflation pressures: the Fed's Millennial problem.

The Millennials' penchant for apartments is one of the more overlooked aspects of the current inflation picture. This preference will have an impact on the Fed and its monetary policy decisions for a long time to come. And it is not a small impact either. Rent and its derivatives constitute roughly 42% of the core inflation, which excludes food and energy, the Fed's preferred measure of CPI.

The quandary is an interesting one, not simply from a demographic standpoint but from the Fed being its own worst enemy in many ways. Multifamily unit starts, a measure of construction activity, has returned to its pre-crisis levels. Arguably, much of this construction was encouraged by low interest rates that forced investors to search for yield. Multifamily projects provided an attractive option.

With the Fed maintaining low rates, developers pushed forward with projects. According to the US Bureau of Economic Analysis (BEA), multifamily investment has never been higher—with the final quarter of 2016 reporting an annualized clip of $62.9 billion. Combined with the National Multifamily Housing Council's survey that found "looser" conditions for the same period, there is an argument to be made that shelter inflation pressures are unlikely to continue levitating and may become a problem for the Fed.

To understand how critical shelter has become to the Fed, it is worth taking a step back to understand the enormity of its influence on inflation. For the twelve months from June 2016 to June 2017, shelter inflation increased at a 3.3% clip. At a 42% weight, shelter's contribution to core CPI is over 1%. Core CPI is increasing at only a 1.7% clip overall. Simply stated, shelter is the inflation story—any deceleration will drive the core rate lower, potentially much lower.

And this is part of the reason why the Fed may have moved too quickly in the first half of 2017. With a low unemployment rate, the combination of infrastructure spending and tax cuts is a classic formula for inflation pressures. But inflation may not be set to accelerate. Instead, it may be set to weaken as shelter becomes a headwind, not the tailwind of the past eight or so years. Not to mention that significant tax cuts do not appear imminent. For the Fed, core CPI may therefore pose a problem to aggressively hiking rates.

If inflation continues to slow, it would be considered a policy error to have raised rates too quickly. But the Fed is running against rent. If shelter does slow toward 1% inflation, it would reduce the contribution to the core to about 0.4% from 1%. That that is more than a half percentage point decline in the core inflation rate. This represents a substantial decline that the Fed would be forced to address.

Imagine the impact if Millennials suddenly begin to want houses. There could be a boom in housing demand with mea-sured shelter inflation falling, even appearing to be deflationary.

How will the Fed react to its Millennial problem? If the emerging inflation pressures turn out to be more misleading than substantial, then the Fed would be forced to back away from its monetary policy plans. This would strengthen the notion that the Fed committed a policy error. For the Fed, the evolution of shelter inflation will be critical. The potential inflationary policies from the Trump administration—tax and regulatory reform—will take time to filter through the economy and may not arrive in time to save the Fed.

It is not difficult to see how the Millennials could ruin the Fed's choice to tighten policy in 2018 and beyond. Granted, rents may continue to rise, but they cannot do so forever. The Millennials matter far more to the Fed than it may care to admit.

The States Are Not Economically Equal

Odd inflation dynamics is not the only difficult piece of US economics with which the Fed will find itself confronted. The US is not economically homogeneous, but it is too often treated as if it were. The US is comprised of regions that have economic spirits all their own. It is unreasonable—though all economists do it—to say, "The US economy is…" anything, because there is no "US" economy.

This regional economic disparity makes it difficult for the Federal Reserve to create effective policies for the country as a whole. By default, the Fed is forced to set policy based on the economies of the larger states. They are the ones that have an effect on the aggregate statistics "US GDP" and "US unemployment." These would be New York, Texas, and California. These three represent about 30% of US GDP. But they are not necessarily representative of the US economy as a whole. This creates the potential for economic overheating in some parts of the country, even while other locales require continued Fed support.

Regionally, the Fed could declare mission accomplished but must remain concerned with developments in lagging regions. Portions of the country have recovered, but the Fed is forced to set monetary policy to produce maximum employment and stable inflation for the whole US. It is an impossible task. It is also one with potential negative consequences for the regions that recover earlier or weather recessionary storms the best. Pockets of the US economy may be allowed to overextend and overheat as the goal of the aggregate is chased with little regard for the local.

This poses a problem: the issue of the aggregate. On the surface, the US is growing at a slow clip with relatively benign inflation. But this hides the potential bubbles that are driving growth. The areas that still languish are shielded by a focus on the singular "US" number. It is nearly impossible to conduct effective regional monetary policy to circumvent these problems. Economists need to be aware of how their policies affect different regions and states and understand that monetary policy for the "US" is a misnomer.

Except for proximity and currency, the economies of US states and regions can have little in common. While the US is a single nation, the US economy needs to be thought of as a collection of smaller, diverse entities. Not a singular whole.

The Engine of Growth

But there is a regional economic heavyweight, and it is the South. It is beginning to look like the economic engine of America. The Census Bureau defines it as from as far west as Texas and Oklahoma, north to Kentucky, east to the District of Columbia and Maryland, down to Florida, and everything in between. This region has come to dominate nearly every economic measure. The South is where the homes are being sold and the jobs are being created. Somehow, while few were watching, the South has become the center of US growth.

The South represents approximately 50% of US housing starts. More than 50% of all single family homes and around 33% of multi-family buildings are started in the South. Even new home sales are more than 50% concentrated in the South, continuing a long rise from the middle of the 20th century. (The

South accounted for 36% of new home sales in 1963.) Existing home sales are much the same story.

The South also generates a relatively high number of jobs. Labor force dynamism is difficult to summarize in a single statistic, but one useful metric is the quits rate—the number of people who quit their jobs as a percent of the overall workforce. A high quits rate is an indication of confidence in labor markets and potentially increasing wage pressures. In fact, the long-term quits rate for the US is 2%. The South at 2.5% is well above the line. The same can be said of hiring. With a 4% hires rate, the South is the most dynamic region on the hiring side as well.

With around 120 million people, the South is the most populous region. While the populations of the Northeast and Midwest regions began to stagnate mid-century, the South and West never stopped growing their headcounts. The South grew its population nearly 50% over the past two decades. This represents about half of all US population growth—more than any other region. (The West grew at a faster clip but contributed less to population growth.)

The fact that the South is where people want to live may have something to do with how far a dollar goes. In 2010, the Census Bureau released its cost of living index, and eight of the 10 cheapest urban areas were in the South. (Four were in Texas.) All 10 of the most expensive cities were in the Northeast and the West with New York and California producing four each. As real wages have been squeezed for the past couple decades, people are searching for a place where their earnings and savings can go farther.

The average new house is larger and cheaper in the South than in any other region. Both average and median home prices are below the other regions. Only the Midwest is close. A slowdown in Southern housing would ripple through the country. After all, the South is half of the market. The health of the US economy may be more closely tied to the South than many observers care to acknowledge—especially those with a "bi-coastal" view of economic activity. In many ways, the US has become reliant on the South to drive the growth for the country. This is especially true post financial bubble, as small fluctuations in demand for housing employment creation could have ripple effects across the entire US economy.

The South is cheap and capitalist—at least, relative to its counterparts in the Northeast and in the West. And sure, the South's economic performance was lifted by an outsized contribution from the Texas oil boom and now that has dissipated. But the South is winning jobs and population and has quietly become the economic driver for the country. The South is rising.

All Bubbles Pop

"All economics are local," the saying (almost) goes. And as should be obvious from the discussion on the diffuse US economy, not all have the same structure. Few people's economic fortunes move in lock step with the United States as a whole. But most feel the push and pull of the local economy. This is where much of the talk about oil has failed. Texas and North Dakota get all the headlines. But other US states suffer much, much more when it comes to falling oil prices.

The vast majority of states do not rely on mining to contribute anything significant to their growth. (In GDP reports, "mining" is the accounting line for oil and gas extraction along with more traditional mining activities.) But there is a handful that rely heavily on it. These are the extraction states, and they have been largely overlooked in the discussion of the oil-price bust.

Yes, oil's decline hurt Texas. But Texas is a state with a somewhat well diversified manufacturing base and other industries cushioned the blow. In 2013—prior to the collapse in oil prices, only about 14% of the economic growth in Texas was directly related to mining. For this and other reasons, the slowdown was manageable. With one of the nation's largest economies, Texas was able to absorb much of the blow, though certain areas of previous rapid growth were severely distressed.

The size of the economies of other states—and their relation to the overall US economy—is relatively small. The effect of significant slowdowns in these states was not felt much in the broader numbers.

For much of the US, the plunge in oil prices was a slight positive, not a negative. But for states that relied heavily on mining for growth, the best times—at least in the near term—are over. North Dakota has been a miracle, and Texas is an enigma.

The Odd Consequences of the Oil Crash

Historically, there would be numerous positives from low oil prices for the US economy. Many of these never materialized and may no longer be relevant at all. The US shale boom, one of the great American growth stories, appears to be over for a while, and the job growth—while no longer falling—has largely dried up. For the traditional oil powers in the Middle East, the harsh reality of low oil will continue to destabilize their region.

The US economy was expected to benefit from lower oil prices. In terms of consumption growth, though, the effects have been minimal. Instead, it appears consumers have used the savings to pay down debt. Instead of spending their oil savings, they are saving it. Undoubtedly, this is necessary, but it fails to show up in present growth rates. Deleveraging bodes well for future growth but does little to thrust the present economy forward. This of course is a bit of a headache for the Fed. Low interest rates are supposed to pull spending forward. Debt was, and remains, cheap. But instead of bingeing on cheap debt—and magnifying the effects with cheap oil—the consumer has turned the other way. This is one of the less publicized and most confounding oddities in the aftermath of the financial crisis.

Maybe households have yet to believe that oil will remain low. Due to constant the rhetoric predicting a recovery in the price from the current $45 to $50 level—and the recent volatility of the price—it may take longer for households to alter their consumption habits. If they ever do. At any rate, the flow of energy savings to the broader economy has lagged. But it is needed for reaccelerating the economy.

This could be a problem, because the US economy does not appear to have the same relationship it once had with high oil prices. Not long ago, higher oil prices threatened to cut economic expansions short. Now the opposite has occurred in the US, as low oil capital expenditures and a strong dollar sent the industrial economy into a recession. The US is a pseudo-petro-state, and as oil patch capital expenditures have fallen, the job losses have followed.

Granted, the overall US jobs picture is quite sanguine, and the losses in the oil patch are a mere blemish. But companies have reacted far more quickly than households and have slashed payrolls accordingly. This leaves the American economy in an intriguing spot, in that a moderate rise in the price of oil may strengthen, not weaken, the US economy.

The Organization of the Petroleum Exporting Countries (OPEC)'s own assumptions for oil demand for the next several decades shows very little growth is expected from the developed world—only 5% total through 2040. Emerging market economies are expected to drive the vast majority of the 49% predicted growth in energy demand.

With most of the economic growth in the past couple decades coming from the emerging world, there are plenty of reasons to believe this will continue. But there are also reasons to be suspicious. In early 2016, the IMF reduced its projected growth rates for the global economy, expecting emerging markets to lag. After all, many emerging market economies were built on high commodity prices. The absence of these creates headwinds for their continued growth and even their medium-term economic and social stability.

Saudi Arabia and Iran's dispute (now spilling into Qatar) and Russia's general discontentment are examples of the geopolitical consequences of lower oil. These situations could flare up, especially if oil prices remain low and strain fiscal budgets. Some countries have cash or capacity to borrow beyond their rivals. This could be the next weapon to maintain market share used by the traditional energy powers. Commodity prices largely determine whether growth comes from the developed world or the emerging world. And oil may be the most important commodity.

Ubering the Economy

Unfortunately for the global economy, the US is grappling with its own labor force issues and how to solve them—and oil played an important role. Enter the Uber economy. Sometimes you need surge pricing and surge pay to balance supply and demand. Uber uses surge pricing (and thus, pay) gets more drivers on the road and makes people think twice before requesting a ride. It also allows the Uber driver to determine to a great extent when, how long, and where they work. Traditional businesses do not have surge pay to adapt to increases in demand and to attract workers. Overtime and signing bonuses do not adjust supply in real time.

Unfortunately, the United States as a whole is not as nimble an operator as Uber. The labor market is an intriguing mix of good and bad news. On the positive side, the unemployment rate is less than 5%, employment is above the pre-Great Recession peak, and employment growth has been steady for years. Yet, the JOLTS report indicates the United States has more than 5 million job openings, and is facing stagnant wage growth. There seems to be phenomena at play not receiving attention: the interaction between the contestability of jobs and the complacency of jobs.

The "complacency of jobs" refers to the lack of incentive to work for lower wages than a worker's perceived skill set deserves. Someone who lost a relatively high-paying job during the Great Recession might be less likely to accept a low wage simply for the sake of having a job. A lack of motivation or holding out for a higher wage may begin to explain the declining unemployment rate and the plummeting labor-force participation rate the United States has today. The lack of financial incentive to take a job leaves both the person out of work (and either in the ranks of the unemployed or out of the labor force) and the company with a job opening. A refusal to work for a perceived low wage should eventually have the effect of pushing wages higher, but this has not been the case so far.

There are other factors working against the numbers as well. In a "normal" economic recovery, there is the expectation that as the labor market tightens, wages increase. This encourages people to switch jobs or even reenter the labor force. Theoretically, the job opening above would increase the salary or hourly wage until it was filled. But wages do not seem to be moving even as the unemployment rate falls. This is why contestability matters.

Jobs are lost en masse during recessions. Companies shed workers to remain profitable (or solvent) in the downturn, and some get hired back. This may be changing, though. As a wide array of US and developed-world jobs come under attack from automation, global high-speed internet connectivity, and the emerging cheap but highly educated labor force willing to perform skilled work for low wages, many people are simply not going to be paid as much to do what they are doing. Labor is being priced on the world market, not the local market. And this suppresses wages below where they would be in a closed economy.

The global economy is setting a wage ceiling for many US jobs, and recruiters and hiring managers understand that many jobs can be filled abroad. The contestability of labor is keeping wages low, even as unemployment falls, because many jobs can be automated or outsourced if wages rise too much. Wages are pressured even as fewer workers are chasing the same job in the United States, because there is a global workforce chasing those jobs as well.

There is another factor at work in the United States: part-time employment and its multi-decade rise as a proportion of the labor force. Typically, the US economy could rely on increased productivity to pick up the slack from fewer workers. The growth equation of more workers making more and more stuff per hour appears to be slowing. The shifting composition of the labor force with more part-time and fewer full-time employees could explain some of the slowdown in productivity. Part-time employees may be less efficient and have lower levels of productivity. And part-time employment increased during the Great Recession and remains high today.

In many ways, the United States is fertile ground for the kind of jobs created by Uber. Uber allows for part-time and flexible hours. The jobs are not contestable (at least until there are self-driving cars). And the complacency factor is counteracted by surge pricing.

In an article concerning inequality, *The Economist* suggested the world is divided "between people who have money but no time and people who have time but no money." Without an emphasis on creating low-contestability jobs (like construction and those in the oil patch—you cannot replace an oil worker with a robot, at least not yet) that are low complacency (oil-field jobs also pay a lot relative to other jobs requiring a similar skill set), it is difficult to see how this trend reverses. Instead, the US labor market is reacting rationally to a changing world—one where wages feel little pressure and people hold out for better jobs. The equilibrium between wages, employment, and participation will eventually be found. For now, though, the United States is becoming increasingly idle.

What Is Made Probably Is Not Counted

Economic output from Uber and similar businesses are difficult for the government to count. Calculating the growth of the US economy has been difficult. The new economy complicates this task even more. GDP is meant to be the singular summarizing statistic of economic growth and prosperity for a nation. It is in fact an inaccurate, untimely, and vague indication of economic activity. "The economy grew at..." should never quote GDP, because GDP does not capture the entirety of economic output.

Illegal activity is also tough to count, but it is economic activity. Some countries in Europe are expanding what is counted in GDP to include drugs and other illegal activities, which boosts their economies by anywhere from 0 to 5%. The oft cited debt-to-GDP ratio will narrow instantly without any change in the financial condition of the government. Of course adding lines to GDP statistics increases the level of GDP, but it does not alter the underlying economy. More stuff gets counted, but nothing has changed in the everyday life of the economy.

What the Europeans are attempting to measure is the informal—the underground—economy. The informal economy is the economic activity not typically measured due to under or unreported income, tax dodging, legality, or otherwise. And it is not trivial. If the European changes were instituted in the US, Eurostat estimates measured US GDP would increase by 3%.

What is the underground economy as a whole hiding? One paper estimates 18%–19% of income is unreported to the IRS. This means that somewhere in the neighborhood of $2.5 trillion is earned off the books. Apply a tax rate of 15% to that figure, and suddenly, $375 billion appears in tax coffers. With the US deficit expected to be $583 billion, it becomes apparent why there is a need to understand the informal economy.

Possibly even more surprising than its size is the fact that the underground economy is not all drug dealers and hedonistic economic participants. California estimated only 15% of the underground is made up of illegal activity. Most of the informal economy is farming, construction, and other forms of easily concealed labor (i.e., workers doing legal things "under the table").

The US has a lot of cash outstanding. This encourages an underground economy. It is difficult to have a vibrant underground economy without cash or another untraceable means of exchange. The government of India took steps to reduce the informal economy by banning large bills. As electronic forms of payment became increasingly popular, it was thought the US would be able to more easily convert informal labor to formal labor. Crypto-currencies, such as Bitcoin, may be a method of building a 21st century informal economy.

And this raises the question of whether the electronic economy can force labor to move to the formal economy. It appears not. The new "micro job" culture is being spurred by innovations in retail and ubiquitous access to the internet. Some of these effects may be showing through the part-time employment figures that have been persistently high over the past decade. Understanding how to convert informal labor market participants into formal ones is critical, simply due to the massive amount of tax revenue at stake.

GDP does a decent job of measuring the size of the formal economy. But it takes some time and a few tries to get there (by the third revision its fairly accurate). As such, it is very useful for understanding, in hindsight, what broad components of the economy drive growth or contraction. But like most economic statistics, GDP means little without the proper context and analysis. It struggles to articulate the finer points of the economic story.

Since GDP is left exclusively to the formal sector, economists, policy makers, and business leaders are not getting the entirety of the economic picture—regardless of the eventual accuracy of the GDP report. Without having some understanding of the informal economy, decision makers are dealing with only a partial picture of GDP, employment, productivity, and wage growth. Measurement of the informal sector may have started with GDP in Europe, but it should continue to other economic measures. (In some cases it already has.)

Granted, if the US were to estimate the informal economy, GDP, employment, and other statistics would likely suffer from larger revisions and decreased accuracy. But we would have a more thorough measure of the output, a more accurate picture of employment, and more insight into how an economy functions. At the moment, the US is measuring only part of the economy and not even doing that very well.

The underground economy is not comprised only of illegal activity, and distortions in the GDP data happen frequently regardless. There are numerous recent examples. For instance, in the aftermath of the Great Recession, economic growth in the fourth quarter of 2009 was entirely due to inventory investment. Change in private inventories (CIPI) contributed 4.4% to GDP, but GDP increased only 3.9%. Other than increasing inventories, the economy shrank by half a percent. It works in reverse as well. In the fourth quarter of 2012, the economy grew only 0.1%, but CIPI was a 1.80% drag. The fundamentals of the economy were performing fine—growing nearly 2%, but inventories distorted away the growth.

It is obvious CIPI poses a problem to understanding what is going on in the underlying economy. Even the Bureau of Economic Analysis (BEA) admits it is incredibly volatile, and that CIPI is difficult to predict. This is a situation similar to the CPI, where economists look at the "core," which excludes the unstable changes in food and energy, to understand its underlying movements. To get a better look at the underlying economy, the BEA does the natural thing. It drops CIPI from the GDP.

The "Real Final Sales of Domestic Product," or Final Sales, figure strips out the effect of CIPI on GDP. In many ways, this resembles more of a "core" GDP than the headline number. The number moves around in much the same way as GDP but tends to be less wild in its movements. While not necessarily a more accurate gauge of economic activity, Final Sales provides more clarity of the underlying economy.

The ease with which most economic data can be misunderstood is astounding. But it is not too difficult to more clearly understand the health of the economy. US data watchers and policymakers should place more weight on this "core" Final Sales GDP. There is an after normal economy in the US. But we do not know how to measure it well.

Janet Yellen Shifts Course... the First Time

Once a year in late August, Federal Reserve policymakers travel to Jackson Hole, Wyoming, to discuss their latest thoughts and papers on monetary policy. In 2016, Federal Reserve Chair Janet Yellen said something remarkable for an economist: The labor market data lacks clarity, is confusing, and is sometimes contradictory. Yellen admitted the Fed is having a difficult time understanding precisely what is happening in the labor markets, and the difficulty of understanding the data has been magnified following the Great Recession. Some variables appear to have lost some of their meaning or "predicative power." But others do not seem to have been affected much at all. This requires a shift in interpreting some data and not necessarily extrapolating past tendencies and correlations to the present.

In the speech, Yellen subtly argued some data her colleagues are relying on should be interpreted with care. Some may not be relaying the same information about the labor market (and output, and wages, and so on) as before the Recession. One to be wary of is the number of people working part time for economic reasons. Yellen points out that there are "structural"—permanent—forces at work here, such as the shift to a services oriented economy where part-time employment is more common. But there is also a "cyclical"—temporary—component, and Fed policy should be effective here.

Remembering back, the Fed has caused itself a problem by stating that monetary policy would be tightened as the unemployment rate dropped and inflation stayed within bounds. And this was causing some issues for Yellen, as some at the Fed believed the unemployment rate—what the Fed tied itself to—was not a good measure of the health of the labor market. So Yellen proffered an idea about how to avoid the problems that using a single data point to determine policy could wreak.

> [I] believe that our assessments of the degree of slack must be based on a wide range of variables and will require difficult judgments about the cyclical and structural influences in the labor market. While these assessments have always been imprecise and subject to revision, the task has become especially challenging in the aftermath of the Great Recession, which brought nearly unprecedented cyclical dislocations and may have been associated with similarly unprecedented structural changes in the labor market—changes that have yet to be fully understood.

The critical element embedded in this statement is the use of a wide range of data to understand an economy vastly different from the one we knew before. To drive her point home, Yellen gives a few examples of what happens when data is not properly understood. Are more job vacancies a good sign for the labor market? Traditionally, yes. After normal, maybe not.

> Given the rise in job vacancies, hiring may be poised to pick up, but the failure of hiring to rise with vacancies could also indicate that firms perceive the prospects for economic growth as still insufficient to justify adding to

payrolls. Alternatively, subdued hiring could indicate that firms are encountering difficulties in finding qualified job applicants.

Job vacancies and hiring are linked. Not understanding this link could render an analysis useless. Or simply looking at the rise in job vacancies could lead to an inaccurate assessment of the labor market and the number of workers being demanded.

Other variables may not be so difficult to understand, even now. The quits rate is one of those. As more people quit their jobs, the better the labor market is assumed to be. It indicates workers' confidence in finding alternative employment and how broadly firms are competing for talent. But as Yellen points out, the quits rate is still "somewhat depressed," and this could be a sign the labor market is not as dynamic as some think. While many of the variables may have been deeply affected by the Recession, the logic behind quitting a job is unlikely to have changed. Not to mention the quits rate is one of the Chair's favorite indicators.

Yellen is a labor economist. This is her territory. It should be disconcerting when she admits there is uncertainty regarding the state of the labor market and how the Fed should react to it. But Yellen did something truly brilliant. Instead of providing economists and Wall Street with specific policy plans, Yellen gave economists and Wall Street a lesson on how to acknowledge a lack of clarity in the data. This may not sound like a monetary policy, but it is. By allowing for uncertainty and calling for a broad range of variables to be used in the determination of policy, Yellen began to allow for almost any policy to be justified by data. After all, the data could be good or bad, but it is certainly indeterminate.

Why Yellen Changed It

The Federal Reserve's mandate has never been well defined. There are no concrete definitions to adhere to. At Jackson Hole in 2016, Federal Reserve Chair Janet Yellen began to deviate from the traditional characterization of full employment—tied to the unemployment rate—to something far more nebulous. Recognizing this shift is critical to understanding the Fed and its new relationship with the two esoteric mandates of stable prices and full employment.

Then, at a conference in Boston, Yellen stated that she was concerned about rising inequality. Before listing a blistering round of statistics indicating the US has become more unequal over the past few decades, Yellen succinctly articulated why the Great Recession was responsible for widening the gap further.

> But widening inequality resumed in the recovery as the stock market rebounded, wage growth and the healing of the labor market have been slow, and the increase in home prices has not fully restored the housing wealth lost by the large majority of households for which it is their primary asset.

One piece in particular of the above statement stands out—and has broad implications for understanding the Fed mandates. A normal recovery would have seen wage growth and the labor market move together in a lagged fashion: The labor market heals and tightens, followed by wage increases as labor becomes increasingly scarce. But this has not happened during the current recovery. And it has not occurred economy wide in quite some time.

The new target for the Fed may be best described as not simply "full employment" but "full wages." At first glance, it seems unreasonable for the chair of the Federal Reserve to be concerned with how the income of the country gets dispersed. However, in many ways, "full wages" are at the intersection of the Fed mandates. In essence, Yellen is admitting that the past few decades were not kind to a significant swath of the US and that this endangers future economic growth.

Many of the jobs US middle skilled workers once took for granted can now easily be outsourced or contested—even some previously thought untouchable. This contestability is increasing as more jobs become relocatable or replaceable due to advances in communications technology. Contestability is fundamental to Yellen's concern. If a US job is contestable internationally, then US workers are competing with cheap labor around the world. As previously mentioned, this limits the bargaining power of the US worker and keeps a lid on wage inflation in the US. The cheap but educated global labor force is becoming an increasing threat to the US worker.

Yellen sees this middle skilled squeeze phenomenon in the data but also sees the lack of deflationary wage pressure on the top of the income ladder. The highest paying jobs tend to have little competition from outside. These jobs are ones that require creativity and high levels of education. The question to ask is why this has occurred and whether the factors underlying it are dangerous to the US economy.

In many ways, they are dangerous. If ignored long enough, the disintegration of the middle class is at best disinflationary and may be deflationary. With stagnant wages across the economy, the middle class cannot increase consumption. One can borrow only so much. If contestability continues to erode the wages of US middle skilled workers, wages could be pressured or even decrease toward more internationally competitive levels. This would be disastrous for consumption and inflation expectations, especially in a service oriented economy where many of the jobs could be at risk.

If the US continues to see this type of wage pressure, there may be enough jobs (for people who want them), but the ability to consume at previous levels will not be there. Deflation—generally—is bad for an economy. Wage deflation might be the worst kind. Deflation puts pressure on prices, making it more difficult to consume on the aggregate as the economy previously did. The standard of living declines. Further, the potential for wage pressures in the current recovery is low. The jobs created during the recovery disproportionately skew toward part-time relative to previous recoveries. And part-time jobs do not yield much bargaining power. There are few reassurances about the labor market.

This puts the Fed in a particularly odd place. Its mandate is supposed to be two separate pieces of a puzzle, but Yellen identified an intersection with a flashing red light. The Fed runs the risk of missing its "full employment" and "stable price" mandates without pursuing—either explicitly or implicitly—a "full wage" target.

Yellen's statement has little to do with fairness or equality. It is directly connected to ensuring the US has created enough uncontestable jobs for the Fed to step away. These jobs are the type that lead to—or at least allow for—future upward wage pressures. Prime examples are the jobs created by the shale oil boom and housing construction during the boom precipitating the financial crisis. Many of the jobs created for the oil patch require the presence of the worker. This makes them difficult to offshore or relocate. As quantitative easing (QE) begins to roll off, the ability of the US shale revolution to stand on its own will be tested, and the jobs engine of Texas may suffer. This would be a tremendous hit to a sector where wage pressures exist and the contestability is low. The Fed should be watching this closely.

Yellen's wage war is a battle the US does not know it must win. For the Fed, it ties together both pieces of its mandate. And it gives them a reasonable basis for stimulus when observers feel it unnecessary. The Fed is muddling the mandate to fight a wage war, but the Fed will struggle to justify its continuous actions to counteract those forces. The middle skills squeeze is not a swiftly passing phenomenon. It may mean that extraordinary monetary policy and unconventional intervention are increasingly normal.

A Step Toward "Normal"?

Much is being made of the Federal Reserve beginning to normalize its policy. It sounds as though the Fed is getting back to its old, boring self. Labor market progress is debatable with a low participation rate, subdued inflation, and lackluster wages. Still, the Fed has ceased its QE stimulus program and raised rates. The federal funds rate, or "fed funds," the primary tool of monetary policy, is still the favored instrument (supposedly). But it remains so low that it is useless as a standalone tool to combat a recession. The theory thus far has been that the US economy can support normalized policy without stumbling—at least too much. It seems the Fed will once again become the dull and subtle institution.

But this is simply not the case. Monetary policy is not going to be "normal" any time soon. Nor is the Fed going to be boring, dull, or subtle. At 1.25%, the fed funds rate must move much higher to reach pre-recession levels. But these levels are unlikely to be seen in the near future. From January 1993 (the trough in fed funds after the 1990 recession) through the end of 2007 (before the Fed dropped it to nearly 0), the monthly average was about 4.4%. To get to that rate again would be no small move and would drastically slow the US economy.

At one point during the post-crisis recovery, the Fed saw rates returning to around 4% in the longer run, but now they see fed funds rates at only around 3% in the long run. The highest projection is now 3.5%. There has been a downward trend in the fed funds rate since the late '70s–early '80s inflation was broken. Each business cycle saw increasingly lower fed funds to combat an economic slowdown, and lower peak rates to cool an expansion. On top of all the other headwinds, this trend is what the Fed is confronting.

Aside from the time it will take to move fed funds back to a more normal level, the side effects of QE will take time to work out. The Fed's balance sheet is currently sitting more than $4 trillion, as QE led to the rapid accumulation of assets.

Much attention has been paid to how quickly the Fed purchased additional assets but little given to the "rolling of maturities." The Fed is currently maintaining the size of its balance sheet by purchasing new securities with the proceeds of those that mature. This keeps the balance sheet the same size but does not increase it. In the future, a critical aspect of Fed guidance will be around the process to shrink it. There are options. The Fed could stop rolling entirely, roll a portion, or maintain the current policy and allow the balance sheet to stay large.

The Fed has stated it intends to reduce the balance sheet to only what is needed to operate (though this will be much higher than before the recession), will hold mostly Treasuries, and will let them roll off. Guidance was only recently provided on when and how rapidly it will reduce the balance sheet. There will be a slowly rising cap on the amount allowed to roll-off,. Any maturities exceeding the cap will be reinvested. The keys that the Fed will be purchasing securities after it begins roll-off its QE purchased assets, and there will be no direct selling. It is a non-aggressive path toward the inflated after normal balance sheet.

It is worth asking whether Fed policy will ever approach something equivalent to a historical norm. For the moment, the answer appears to be no—at least for a very, very long time. Even if the Fed continues to raise fed funds moderately over the next couple years, it is unlikely it will be able to move them higher quickly enough to get them "back to normal" in any real way. There is also the question of how effective monetary policy can be in this type of environment. If there is a shock to the economy in 2018 and the fed funds rate is sitting at 1.5%, how will the Fed react? With little room to move rates lower, the Fed would likely be forced to resort to QE or even a negative interest rate policy—or the threat of it. Unconventional monetary policy is much more conventional in the after normal economy.

The Fed may have ended QE, but this does not mark the end of the unconventional era. Ignoring that central banks in

Europe and Asia are using negative rates, the Fed itself has little chance of going back to normal. The balance sheet will remain inflated for a long time—long after the Fed begins to reduce it. The US will likely see QE in the (near) future to stimulate the economy as moving the fed funds rate has less of an effect trapped too close to 0%. The Fed, a once simple to understand institution—moving interest rates up or down—has become an increasingly difficult one to predict. Monetary policy may someday return to the simplicity of old, but normal will not return any time soon.

The Fed Fights for Texas

It is worth rewinding a bit to understand the stimulative power of QE. There is no doubt the Federal Reserve's QE policy influenced markets both at home and abroad. But it seems even policy makers may have misinterpreted the precise channels through which it would affect the US economy. Certainly, lower interest rates lower are part of the attention, and the Fed appears to have succeeded there. But interest rates are only one transmission mechanism. And QE may well have worked much better than even Fed officials want to believe it did.

There are myriad suggestions about the transmission mechanisms through which QE works. (Some would debate whether it works at all.) But it is now generally accepted that QE played a primary role in driving down the value of the US dollar prior to 2014. This happens as investors search for better returns in their portfolios of risk assets. Money flows to countries with relatively higher yields and returns, and away from countries with lower yield. This is one mechanism driving the real exchange rate of a country's currency—in this case the US dollar—lower.

Raghuram Rajan, the head of the Reserve Bank of India, stated at the Brookings Institution in April 2014 that "some advanced economy central bankers have privately expressed their worry that the QE 'works' primarily by altering exchange rates...." In other words, without the effect that QE has on exchange rates—lower for the US dollar—there may not be much of an effect at all. Regardless of whether or not the statement is entirely accurate, this is a far more significant admission than it initially appears.

If a significant portion of the Fed's QE effect was pushed through the exchange-rate channel, this has implications for assets priced in US dollar terms. As the dollar declines, commodities become less expensive in non-dollar terms. This means commodities are cheaper in yen or euros. This stimulates demand for commodities in non-dollar countries, and this in turn causes prices of those commodities to rise in dollar terms as demand increases.

The weakening dollar did not have a direct impact on US buyers. But it had an indirect one by stimulating demand for it. The effect of a weaker US dollar on the price of commodities can be substantial. Granted, there were also supply and demand forces driving oil prices, but changes in the value of the reserve currency accentuates the price movement.

So, QE is meant to spur domestic demand for assets and increase consumption by increasing the size of the Fed's balance sheet as it purchases securities or targets specific rates. It is also likely that the highly accommodative Fed policy resulted in a dollar that was weaker than it otherwise would have been. And the unintended impact of the easing was a depreciating dollar, which led to commodity prices that were more expensive in dollar terms.

In essence, the Fed waged a trade war. QE held the value of the dollar down, which stimulated demand for commodities and eventually increased their price. And it made massive US shale production possible and profitable or at the very least made more wells more profitable. Admittedly, it is not simply a weakened dollar that enabled the US energy renaissance, but it certainly helped. QE also helped to maintain a high price during a period of relatively meager and stagnant global economic growth. This may also be a decisive component of the recovery, and the Fed is overlooking it. QE caused more hiring in the oil sector than would have otherwise been, increased profits domestically, and propped up emerging market growth through the commodity price channel.

Unsurprisingly, the Fed is not about to admit that it waged a trade war. And this may be one of the few times the Fed gets away with it. After all, QE was supposed to lower interest rates, not alter the global commodity-production landscape. The other reason is that lower-cost Mideast oil was replaced with higher-cost US oil. Domestic oil production creates US jobs and keeps the US trade balance in better shape.

But there is a problem. QE came to an end, caused the dollar to strengthen, and oil prices declined. Typically, this would be good for the US consumer. Lower oil prices are similar to a tax cut allowing them to shop and go out to eat more. But this time it did not play out like previous episodes. Instead, consumers saved and the economy gained little.

The Fed had only a couple areas of high growth: the shale boom and Silicon Valley. And as the Fed moved closer to raising rates, it mistook these pockets of growth for a broader and deeper recovery. This was a misinterpretation of the situation. Raising rates—more specifically, halting QE—caused the value of the dollar to increase and contributed to the downturn in the price of oil. But the Fed has to deny its involvement in higher oil prices from the beginning. The strong dollar and oil glut caused significant damage to the growth engine of the US economy—not to mention the broader consequences of low oil prices globally. Fed officials should be more concerned with the unintended fallout of their actions and less worried about how to properly word their press releases.

Without realizing it (or admitting it), the Fed fought and won a trade war, since QE held the dollar down and the price of oil up. It is not a coincidence that QE and the shale boom ended at the same time. The Fed misread why the US economy appeared to be ready for less QE. And the unintended impact of QE may actually have been the most effective. At any rate, it is becoming increasingly evident that unconventional monetary policy creates outcomes far beyond those that are intended.

The Global Economy and the Fed... Before the Trap

The Fed has been accused, among many other things, of ignoring the global economy. Vice Chairman Stanley Fischer would beg to differ. In a speech in early October 2014 to the IMF, Fischer was clear in his claim the Fed does include global economic outcomes in its analysis. And this is a good thing. More than that, in a world where the US dollar dominates the financial landscape, it is a must.

But attempting to normalize with most of the developed world moving in the opposite direction creates frictions. The Fed found it tough to account for and anticipate the Bank of Japan's typical surprise monetary policy maneuver with a QE package. And the ECB attempting to spur economic growth and inflation in the eurozone with QE and ever deeper negative interest rates was also tough. China's devaluation, rate cutting, and fiscal stimulus to stem their economic slowdown added to the complication of policy. The monetary policy actions in 2014-2015 by the Fed were difficult on their own, and made far more difficult by the actions of other central banks.

The Fed, when it ended QE, handed the direction of the global economy to other central banks who took the opportunity to stimulate their own economies. If the world's central banks become increasingly loose with their monetary policy, the discussion shifts from the unintended impact of Fed policy to the possible outcomes based on the decisions of the rest of the central banks. The Fed's policy of QE-forever-if-needed inspired other central banks to undertake similar actions. This is especially true since those other banks are less concerned with domestic economic health and more about currency competitiveness.

Central banks could legitimately argue that this is not unlike what the US did for the past decade or so. According to Fischer's statement: 1) The Fed is concerned about the potential spillover effects of its policy (both during and after its implementation) in the currency and bond markets. 2) The Fed should step in to do something if it is needed for global financial stability and by consequence, the US economy, 3) which is part of the Fed's mandate. The Fed is obviously aware and ready to counteract the effects of its choices on the rest of the world. But is it ready to consistently counteract the effects of the rest of the world on the US?

The decisions of the rest of the world—especially those of the larger, developed world central banks—directly affect economic outcomes in the US. And the Fed is paying attention. Fischer said as much, well before the Fed began to cite the global economy in its FOMC press releases.

> In determining the pace at which our monetary accommodation is removed, we will, as always, be paying close attention to the path of the rest of the global economy and its significant consequences for US economic prospects.

But the Fed is unlikely to base policy on such considerations—at least until things get out of control and begin to influence economic outcomes. The beginning of 2016 was such a time. The Fed raised rates in December 2015, and the Chinese markets tumbled spilling into the US. The fallout was combatted by the Fed backing away from the previous pace of tightening. Instead of three hikes in 2016, the Fed raised once. A far slower pace than initially anticipated. This shifted the Fed from a US data and potential outcomes stance to a reactive stance based on foreign central bank moves.

The problem? It was difficult to stem the shift once it began. Once the Fed implicitly tied itself to global economic conditions and not solely the US, markets began to pay far closer attention to global stability than before. US monetary policy was essentially hamstrung.

The Fed has another problem: the strong dollar. Excessive US dollar strength jeopardized many of the positive US growth stories. And it made the US even less globally competitive in manufacturing. Lower transport costs (due to low oil prices) further weakened it. As cheaper goods began to flow into the country from abroad, prices are held down—and thus the US imported at least some deflation. In these ways and more, the rest of the world had a real, tangible effect on the US. Not to mention they threaten to dislodge market participants' faith in the Fed's ability to stem disinflation or even the possibility of deflation.

So, in the post-QE era, the Fed is forced to shift its focus from mostly or only internal forces to external ones. With particular attention to the big three central banks and the spillover effects their policies have on the US economy. According to Fischer, this should not worry onlookers. But he was more concerned with the US effect on economies abroad, not their effect here. This was wishful thinking. And he left the door open to taking the global economy into account when determining policy. He even stated that global financial stability was consistent with the Fed's mandate.

With Fischer looking abroad at spillover effects and Yellen looking internally at inequality, the Fed's mandate is becoming convoluted and far more difficult to understand. The Fed let go of the lead in global easing, and there were consequences. The US could afford a stronger dollar for a while, but not forever. Fischer, when building his case for the Fed to be more global-looking, cited economist Charles Kindleberger's theory that the global economy would benefit from a hegemonic central bank. Fischer retreated from this idea, insisting the Fed did not view itself this way. But maybe it should. The dollar *is* the world currency for now. The Fed cannot afford to lose control of it.

Losing It

Even after surviving several rate increases, any mention of tightening evokes memories of the "taper tantrum" and the December 2015 hike with its ensuing volatility. But before he Fischer doctrine of looking abroad had yet to take hold at the Fed, emerging market currencies were sent into tailspins in 2012 when then-Fed Chair Ben Bernanke stated the Fed would begin tapering and again after the December 2015 rate increase. The Fed assumed global central banks were prepared for such action. In both cases, they were not, and considerable economic damage was done.

The US is the "consumer of first resort" for the global economy. So, countries it has good trade relations benefitted from a stronger dollar. As the dollar appreciates, it makes the US market more attractive to exporters. Because the prices of goods and services have increased in their local currency, foreign companies can cut prices and still generate as much, if not more, revenues. This, however, causes US firms to cut prices and requires job cuts and other measures to maintain profitability. Price cutting puts downward pressure on inflation. And job cuts put downward pressure on economic growth. These are not enjoyable occurrences for the US economy.

Inflation expectations—what people expect inflation to be in the future—are a large factor in the determination of interest rates (at least theoretically). Low inflation, and especially falling inflation expectations, combined with low growth means investors demand less return for their "risk free" investment, US government debt. With US growth expected to be around only 2% and inflation barely at—or below—the Fed's 2% target, investors have been willing to accept a 10-year US Treasury yield of less than 2%. With oil below $50 per barrel and a strong dollar, inflation may be difficult to find regardless of the relative strength of the US economy.

The non-commodity dependent emerging world should benefit from a stronger dollar and resilient US consumer market. The US should be able to do well without the rest of the world for a while. But it may not last. After all, there is not much in the way of a manufacturing economy remaining in the US. What does remain is stiff competition and not easily challenged by foreign competitors on the basis of price. There have been some manufacturing side effects, but services—the main employer of the US economy—have been resilient.

All else equal, as the dollar appreciates, commodities become more expensive in non-dollar terms—destroying demand. This places emerging market economies with commodity exposure in a particularly vulnerable position to a prolonged or sharp depreciation of their currency. And more than a few sharp depreciations were witnessed in the years following the oil collapse. Currency depreciation risks sparking inflation with imported goods becoming expensive quickly. It is a difficult scenario to escape without higher interest rates and the potential for a painful recession. This is the commodity world's stagflation trap.

The Fed is in a tough position. Its main policy mechanism of raising short-term interest rates has little effect on interest rates farther out the yield curve—especially with inflation expectations falling. For the foreseeable future, he Fed has little room to move interest rates lower before it is forced to move to less conventional measures. Because of this the Fed cannot be too aggressive in a falling or low inflation environment. And fed funds can rise only so much more before the curve would be "flat." That tends to be indicative of a recession. In other words, the Fed is limited (to a degree) by forces out of its control. Namely, falling oil prices and other developed market central banks with loose though no longer loosening policy.

These initially acted in concert to push the dollar higher and inflation expectations lower. The Fed's decision to begin normalization of QE had its primary impact through the currency market. The dollar gained value quickly. Luckily for the Fed, the dollar has begun to reverse course in 2017. There was the potential for the strong dollar development to haunt the US as weaker inflation expectations create a feedback loop that forces ever slower policy changes. The Fed knows there will be some fallout to raising interest rates and is likely to do so anyway. The plan may backfire on the US

Sometimes, it is worth leaping into the unknown—such as with QE. With inflation and inflation expectations slipping, tightening monetary policy is an experiment with delayed consequences. The dollar may prove to be the mechanism that will come back to haunt the Fed. And it may not take a considerable time for it to happen.

The Problem of Oil and the Dollar

While the dollar is no longer appreciating, the dollar's value has appreciated significantly over the past few years. Historically, there are a few other examples but not many of comparable size and voracity. The unprecedented climb in the early '80s and the dollar's run in the late '90s, for example. The steepness and rapidity of the 2014 to 2016 dollar appreciation made it difficult for firms to react. And this was a problem.

On the surface, this appears to be fairly simple macroeconomics. As the dollar appreciates, imports rise and export volumes come under pressure. And the trade balance deteriorates. However, global trade has become far more complex over the past couple decades as multinationals diversified their supply chains globally. The assumption that foreign firms gain from an appreciation in the dollar still generally holds true to a degree, but many foreign firms have moved portions of their production to the United States. By manufacturing in the US, foreign firms miss some of the advantages of a depreciating currency.

For a moment, foreign firms producing goods in their home country and selling them to the United States have a distinct advantage. The translation of a dollar sale into their domestic currency instantly appears as a gain. They did not raise their price to the US consumer but still got more of their own currency.

The currency mechanism at work here is referred to as "pass-through." It leaves firms—both domestic and foreign—with difficult decisions to make. For the foreign firm, the question is whether to lower their prices to gain market share. The foreign firm gains from the depreciation of its currency but also gains from undercutting the domestic firm's pricing and seizing market share.

For the domestic firm, the decisions are more painful. The domestic firm does not have the benefit of translating the currency and receiving a paper gain. Instead, domestic firms are forced to react to the low pricing from foreign competitors in their domestic markets and absorb a portion of their currency appreciation when selling abroad (or be forced to raise prices). Neither of these are positives for the domestic economy. Firms forced to cut price tend to cut people as revenues and profit margins come under pressure. This is the ugly side of an appreciating currency: the importation of deflation alongside wage and employment pressures.

And falling oil prices do not help.

It is worth noting the rally in the dollar that started in mid-2014 and peaked in 2016 was partly due to the relative strength of the US economy, allowing monetary policy in the United States to become less accommodative than most other developed countries. This divergence tends to strengthen the dollar. But US economic growth was driven only by a boom in domestic oil production and a few other bright spots like Silicon Valley—not an all-around vibrant economy. The oil price plummet and lack of a steady recovery has reminded many that oil is highly cyclical, even shale. Previously, the United States may have benefitted from a stronger dollar through lower input prices and lower transportation. But now, more and more oil is domestically produced, and the associated costs are in US dollars.

The US economy was supposed to benefit from an increase in consumer spending to offset the losses of jobs and the corresponding capital expenditures in the oil patch. But these gains have been offset to some extent by the dynamics of imports and exports. Typically, it would have come with a lag. This time around, however, the effects appear to be flowing through to the real economy much more swiftly. The combination of lower oil and an appreciating dollar was felt in slow US growth. And the pressures will continue to wax and wane as the Fed shifts its expectations.

The US continued to outperform the rest of the world economically, but there was a cost for domestic firms. Corporate profits were pressured as oil fell and competition increased only recovering in 2017. With little growth in their home markets, foreign firms seek out a place to sell. The combination of an appreciating dollar and strong economy are far too enticing. If the dollar resurges, the durability of the US economy will be tested and to a greater extent than some people anticipate. Low oil prices and a higher dollar may be a positive for the economy in terms of consumer consumption. But in the aggregate, the US may find itself under a renewed competitive threat.

It May Not Get Better Quickly

Most analysts seem to be concentrating on the supply side of the oil-price equation. US shale and unconventional sources have the potential to provide incremental supply to the markets. But there is also something else at work: demand. Demand growth has been taken for granted for the better part of the 21st century.

China built infrastructure and its economy grew, which created more demand for oil, and the cycle repeated. Now demand growth is more tenuous and price sensitive. The familiar refrain, "Oil cannot stay cheap forever," may be true. But it can stay low for a while.

There are numerous oddities in the oil market. Chief among them is that oil is a dollarized commodity. And this means the US dollar has a direct effect on the price of oil—specifically in non-dollar terms. This implies that the dollar's strength matters for oil's price recovery, because it can dramatically affect the price that non-US buyers must pay without the dollar price of oil actually moving.

What happened in the fall of 2014 and winter of 2015 was a perfect storm for oil. Not only did the US dollar rise, but oil supplies rose. Both had the effect of pushing prices lower. As the value of the dollar rose, it caused oil to be relatively more expensive to non-US buyers in their domestic currencies. Imagine a euro bought $1.25 and this suddenly fell to $1.00. An $80 barrel of oil would go from costing €64 to €80 without the dollar price moving at all. Essentially, the fall in oil prices allowed the dollar to strengthen without causing the price of oil to rise in non-dollar terms.

Price sensitivity makes this dynamic more interesting. Since oil fell and the US dollar rose, the initial effects outside the United States were marginal. If there is a 30% rise in the dollar and a 30% slump in crude prices, a foreign currency buys about the same amount of oil as before.

Back in reality, the US dollar strengthened significantly as the Fed moved away from its easing policy in mid-2014. The dollar moved due to a confounding mix of policy tightening through the tapering of QE and only a slightly higher fed funds rate. Furthermore, this increased the already volatile so-called forward guidance, the practice of the Fed telling markets what it intended to do. All this while maintaining a modicum of stimulus through the maintenance of its bloated balance sheet.

But while the Fed was engaging in semi-controlled monetary-policy chaos, other foreign central banks were clearer with their intentions. Their message: "There will be quantitative easing and there will be lots of it." Japan and the EU both launched or renewed QE campaigns to spur inflation. China has also stepped up its pace of policy easing, though not through the use of QE. In the end, all of this served to strengthen the US dollar. There is little to suggest that other central bank policies will drastically change soon. There is always chatter of the potential conclusion of their stimulus programs, but thus far it remains only chatter.

Oil at $40 to $50 per barrel is cheap compared to recent norms. This causes some confusion in price expectations. Analysts and commentators feel as though it *should* be more expensive. But the marginal demand is coming from outside the United States. It is the non-dollar cost that matters for demand creation.

And this is an unintended side effect of the Fed's deviation from the easing policies of other central banks. Oil prices cannot easily recover without a change in course. Demand could be stifled by a further and sustained strengthening of the dollar.

Looking forward, the Fed is suggesting it will continue to tighten. The questions of how far and how fast the dollar will move depend on the interaction of Fed policy with those of other self-concerned policy making bodies. But all else being equal, the dollar should remain relatively strong as Fed policy deviates further and further. This causes a new dilemma for those who believe oil will sustainably recover to near prior levels: How can dollar oil prices increase significantly when the dollar is strong?

If the dollar does rise, it is a de facto increase in the price of oil for the rest of world (unless the price of oil falls in an offsetting manner). In short, the Fed is an unwilling linchpin in the oil-price game, and the Fed's future interest-rate decisions will have an effect on how the oil recovery unfolds.

And it is not simply the lynchpin in a vague, theoretical sense either. In early 2016, when the Fed backed away from its path of easing to a slower and more gradual path, the dollar fell and oil rose. There were other factors involved, certainly, but the fall in the dollar assisted in pushing the commodity from its lows. While counterintuitive, an oil recovery may be what the US economy needs to emerge for its growth quagmire.

Higher Oil May Be Better Oil

Plummeting oil prices were initially cheered. In 2016, many observers thought oil may have bottomed, possibly marking the beginnings of a comeback. The vaunted "tax break" to consumers from lower gasoline prices and heating fuel, and its potential positive economic effects, were waning. But the US economy realized little of the expected benefits from lower oil. And awkwardly, high oil prices may actually be a good thing for the US economy.

To date, lower oil prices have not been all that helpful. This should not be surprising. For a decline in oil to matter, it is not enough for the price of oil to fall. Before consumers are willing to spend the "gasoline stimulus," they need to have confidence lower oil prices will stay low. It needs to remain low. Or, at least, that is the common economic logic.

Oil have been low enough for long enough that the effects should have filtered into the economy. But the US economy not only has yet to feel the stimulus, the consumer boom is nowhere to be found. There is some evidence households are using the savings on health insurance and to pay down debt but little evidence that it is increasing economic growth. What happens when households begin to believe that oil is past its lows?

Part of the lack of a low oil dividend may simply be that households are harder to convince today than in previous cycles. The economic rhetoric has been focused on the increasing demand from developed markets, and oil prices have been very volatile over the past 10 years. Due to the rhetoric and how volatile the price of oil has been lately, it may take longer for households to alter their consumption habits.

There are a few notable pieces of data that saw a boost from low oil prices. Consumer sentiment indicators are elevated and near pre-recession highs. Some of this is likely due to lower oil prices. Some is also due to lower unemployment and the perception of a stable economic environment. But all things considered, lower oil prices did not benefit the underlying US economy to the extent economists thought it would.

Oil prices were volatile in the previous decade. The price moved more than higher by 700% between November 2001 and August 2008. That was followed by a 75% precipitous decline in four months, an approximate 250% gain in two years, and then a 75% drop in 18 months. It is not an unreasonable expectation that households may require longer time periods to trust low oil prices will remain depressed. Or simply never believe it.

The US economy does not have the same relationship it once had with high oil prices. Not long ago, higher oil prices threatened to cut short economic expansions. Presently and to the contrary, the US has now become a pseudo-petrostate, and oil patch job losses came swiftly as the rig count fell. Companies react far more quickly than households, and they slashed payrolls quickly. It could get worse, but the US economy has already felt some of the possible pain of oil's downside.

Higher oil prices allowed a number of US regions to grow quickly. These regions drove much of the growth in the US economy out of the Great Recession. As oil fell, so did the growth rates in the regions. Texas gets much of the attention, but others have greater concentrations of oil for their growth. The reason Texas gets much of the attention is simply its size, recent rapid GDP growth, and steady employment gains. The shale boom was a significant boost to the economic recovery, and its absence was felt acutely.

As a consequence, the US economy is not only unlikely to ever truly benefit from but has already felt much of the pain of lower oil prices. This leaves the US economy in an intriguing position. Households have not spent the savings, so an oil prices increase would not be the typical headwind to growth. Instead, reasonably higher prices would stem the job losses in the oil sector without damaging the consumer much. This dynamic places the US economy in a strong position to handle higher oil prices. In fact, a moderate rise in the price of oil may strengthen, not weaken, the US economy. $70 may be the new $40.

Beating the Saudis

When Saudi Arabia decided to wage a war on US shale and other high cost oil producers, it understandably underestimated the resilience of American industry. Now, backtracking, Saudi Arabia has led members of OPEC to scale back production in an effort to increase oil prices. Shale appears to be the nemesis that will not retreat.

For Saudi Arabia and other oil-dependent countries, the failure to break US shale quickly and easily is both disheartening and indicative of an uncertain future. Oil is plentiful—and potentially economical—in places previously thought to no longer be cost effective. This changes the math for winning and losing in the oil market. With its capitalist underpinnings, US shale has the dynamism to compete with the larger, far less efficient state-owned enterprises that dominate much of the competitive landscape.

The shift was not simply a product of technological advances and cost cutting but also the ability to finance money-losing operations. Blame could be heaped on the Fed for causing yield-starved investors to keep "zombie" oil companies afloat. Given the low interest rate environment, investors were willing to finance companies that, in normal interest rate environments, would have been shunned.

This provided an extension of life that may not have been available without the Fed's policy. But the complete picture of how shale producers in the US managed to survive—not all, but many—is far more complicated. Shale did not come out of the downturn unscathed, and the Saudi Arabia-led assault was successful in pushing many less profitable or marginal producers out of the market. According to Fitch Ratings, $38 billion in defaults occurred in 2016. While the industry survived, there was significant carnage beneath the surface. And while the worst is likely over, there is still some pain to be felt.

But the Federal Reserve's role in the oil-price game goes farther than simply causing investors to take more risks. To a certain degree, the Fed helped build the US shale industry in the first place. The Fed's monetary policy decisions affect the value of the dollar. And the value of the dollar affects the price of oil. With the Fed undertaking unconventional policies and pumping money into the economy, the US dollar lost value. This helped drive up prices. With high oil prices, US shale was profitable, and drilling surged. Low interest rates to borrow and drill, combined with high oil prices, were a boon to the US shale industry.

In some ways, it was also a curse. The tailwinds of a weak dollar and strong prices reversed quickly. This caused problems for the debt-laden producers. The Fed, directly responsible for the strength of the dollar, tapered quantitative easing and subsequently began to raise rates slowly starting in the middle of 2014. The combination of a stronger dollar, an oil glut from US shale, and consistent pumping from OPEC nations sent crude oil prices plummeting. Little could be done to halt the fall. Someone had to blink.

With the November 2016 agreement to cut production, OPEC blinked first. Many OPEC nations are entirely dependent on oil revenues to fund their governments. The consequences associated with the default of a small or medium sized exploration and production company are far less severe than the impact of a sovereign nation failing to deliver transfer payments to citizens. One is a bankruptcy proceeding, the other is a civil war.

But can US shale's comeback (or continued resiliency) be sustained? The answer is a resounding "probably." The tailwinds of a weak—or dramatically weakening—dollar have only recently become a potential tailwind as 2017 saw the dollar begin to fall. But even so the dollar remains at an elevated level. The Fed is tightening slowly and unlikely to accelerate the pace much for fear of squelching already tepid inflation. So the Fed and the dollar are neither friend nor foe. Not the best position to be in, but there are worse ones.

OPEC also seems reluctant to willing allow oil to remain at such low prices. This may change, but for now at least, it is constructive for oil prices at some point in the future. Because oil prices are under pressure from multiple angles, there is little ability for OPEC to alter the trajectory immediately. Growth in the demand for oil and its derivatives is coming under pressure as more fuel-efficient vehicles and other forms of transportation become available or mandated. Supply is not lacking as production becomes economical through improving technology and falling costs. These are not temporary.

US shale felt the pain of lower prices but was not broken. Instead, OPEC and Saudi Arabia blinked first. In many ways, this is the second coming of shale. In other ways, it never went away.

Maybe the US Should Limit Oil Imports

But there are things that can be done to push oil prices higher and create jobs in the US. The Trump administration was whisked into office on the back of a nationalistic, blue-collar rhetoric. Trump promised better jobs and wages for the American worker. Trade deals and the offshoring of manufacturing to other countries, it was frequently stated or implied, have led to the demise of the American worker and the American Dream. This may well be true, but identifying the problem and solving it are two different things.

Most of the manufacturing jobs are not coming back to the United States. The manufacturing itself might, but it is unlikely to bring many jobs along with it. Another overly ambitious campaign promise then?

Manufacturing jobs are difficult to replace. Not only are the wages high, but the educational attainment needed for traditional manufacturing roles is minimal. A high school education and a good manufacturing role could, once upon a time, maintain a middle class lifestyle. There are few professions with similar dynamics.

One of them is oil. More specifically, oil-field jobs are high-paying jobs that are vulnerable to market cycles and available to workers without significant education. Granted, as the technology changes, the educational requirement to be a field hand may as well. Just like the manufacturing jobs of old. Construction employment would also fit the mold, but that is somewhat difficult to spur. (Although Greenspan and the housing boom tell a different tale.)

Another oil boom, however, would require elevated prices or a technological leap to reduce extraction costs even further. The first does not seem likely given that the world is awash in crude and not even OPEC has been able to get oil prices sustainably higher. The second is unforeseeable. It could happen, but there is no way of knowing when it would happen.

Higher oil prices, then, would seem to be the one way to guarantee that blue-collar jobs will be created. But for most of America, higher oil prices are wholly unacceptable. Seeing prices at the pump rise evokes images of dollars vanishing overseas and diminished spending power from the American public. The conventional logic of the US economy holds that higher oil prices are bad, and lower prices are good.

But as we have seen in previous pages, that logic is flawed. The United States has emerged as an energy superpower. This has altered its relationship to oil prices. Some of the US' best growth rates during the recovery were recorded when oil was $100—not when oil was $30. Not to mention the fact that when oil prices fall and US workers lose jobs, those jobs are being sent to low-cost producers overseas. This is not dissimilar to the off-shoring of manufacturing jobs. In early 2017, researchers from the University of Notre Dame and the University of Michigan found evidence that increases in oil investment due to rising oil prices will offset the economic impact of reduced consumer spending. This should have been obvious, but it was not.

So what should be done? How does the United States take advantage of its energy superpower status and create an economic and employment opportunity out of it? Simply, the US should limit the importation of foreign crude oil.

The Saudis have already announced that they will ship less crude oil to the United States. This is not a magnanimous attempt to generate jobs on American shores but rather an attempt to speed the consumption of the stockpiles that the United States has built up over the past couple of years. The Saudis would likely view a cap on US exports as constructive, not destructive to the oil market.

Limiting crude imports would be a blunt instrument and inherently controversial. After all, the United States is not yet comfortable in its skin as an energy superpower. The idea that higher oil prices might boost economic growth is the antithesis of the postwar mindset. But it may indeed be the case.

Using some rough figures for illustration purposes, assume the US consumes about 20 million barrels of oil per day and produces around nine million. If the United States slowly began to implement an import cap, then oil prices would rise and induce domestic production increases. Again, the idea is to encourage domestic production, not to shock the economy with far higher oil prices.

Executed properly, this could act as a price-floor mechanism. By keeping prices at a reasonable level—say $70—US energy companies could make long-term investments knowing that their home market would support them. That leads to investments in people, technology, and projects that would otherwise struggle. A moderate price increase would benefit—not endanger—the consumer economy of the United States.

The worry would be that prices might rise too quickly. But shale reacts quickly to incentives. This would keep a slowly increasing limit on crude imports from shocking the system. Another concern is the impact to the so-called "petrodollar." This is the dollarized system of crude-oil purchases globally. Capping US imports will certainly have the effect of lowering the dollar's global role. But it will be minimal relative to other factors in determining the dollar's lasting prominence.

If the US wants to create high paying and easily attainable jobs, then the obvious target is crude oil and its related manufacturing sectors. A cap on imported oil will encourage domestic investment and hiring and speed the rebalancing of global supply and demand. The major oil producers are already attempting to do exactly that. So there should be few aggravated counterparties.

Not long ago, the United States had strict export policies on oil. Now it should be the opposite. In an age where middle skilled jobs are scarce, oil is an option the United States cannot squander. It is time to make oil great again.

Here's How It All Goes Down

Unlike the situation in the 1970s, oil is not going to be the next great shock to send the US down. So, what is likely to cause the next recession? There are always threats to US economic growth.

Much of the time, the derailment comes from unanticipated events, but there are a few persistent headwinds that could spill over to the US economy.

China, officially growing at 6.9% annually, has a debt problem, and—increasingly—a growth problem. According to the Boston Consulting Group, as wages rise and internet speed becomes a more important factor, the US is becoming increasingly competitive with China. But this is the least of China's worries. For China, a strengthening US dollar alleviates some of this pressure but not much, given the renminbi (RMB) peg to a "basket of currencies". Because of this, the RMB has not fallen much against the dollar, so little benefit has accrued to the Chinese economy. For now though, the primary concern is the outflow of wealth from China, and a stable RMB may help alleviate some of this pressure.

China is attempting to pivot its economy from manufacturing and infrastructure to a higher proportion of internal consumption growth. The question is whether China can complete this transition without a significant blow to the global economy. The answer, unfortunately, is that this seems unlikely. China's growth matters, because even if its growth significantly decelerates from current levels, China's economy will contribute more than $1 trillion to global GDP and more than 20% of all global growth on a purchasing power parity basis. Even though the Chinese economy is slowing, it is still a juggernaut.

If the Chinese economy were to undergo a hard landing, global economic growth would come to a standstill or—more likely—shrink. US trade partners, including Canada and Australia, would struggle. And the feedback to the US would be felt in everything from corporate earnings to employment to financial-system pressures. As the driver of much of the marginal global economic growth, China is particularly important for the incremental global worker hired and the incremental widget sold. A substantial, prolonged period of low Chinese growth would likely pull the United States into a recession or a period of prolonged below-trend growth: the speed of economic growth seen in the US of late.

The direct financial links between China and the US financial system are minimal. So, even if a Chinese debt crisis does erupt, it will be felt only minimally directly from China. But there are significant *indirect* linkages through US trading partners, business credit extended by US corporations to aid business growth, and general trade growth. The US housing crisis caused a contagion that spread to Europe from the United States. With China, a problem could flow through the European ties to the United States. Financial markets would react negatively and safe-haven assets—already trading at historic levels in much of the world—would see even greater demand. This could potentially cause havoc for other asset prices.

For the US, the problem with a Chinese debt crisis is the dramatic drop in economic activity it would cause. So, it would have both a financial market impact and a real-economy impact. Much like the financial crisis of 2008. China's economy shrinking would be a shock to the global system as its contribution of $1T in economic growth to the global economy will be difficult, if not impossible, to replace.

Another way the global economy could find itself mired in a downturn is the myriad crises that seem to emanate from Europe with regularity. To say the least, Europe still has an integration problem. The disparate nature of the individual countries' economies makes the ECB's job an impossible task. Choosing between the wants of Germans and the wants of Greeks creates a political situation out of one that should be based on the economic outcomes.

This politicization of monetary policy—Germany accusing the ECB of overheating its economy—is an issue. Instead of providing stability in times of economic strife, the central bank—in this case the ECB—may become a source of volatility and instability as it attempts to balance the needs of some with the wants of others.

If the persistent fears surrounding the EU's eventual collapse become reality, there would be repercussions for the rest of the world. There are the obvious financial issues. For instance, would the remaining highly indebted nations of Europe be able to borrow without the implicit backing of the ECB? But there are also the less obvious global economic effects. Despite struggling for the better part of the last decade, Europe's economy is second only to the US', and it dominates trade with both China and the US. Both the US and China would suffer significantly with faltering demand as the EU broke up.

A breakup of the EU would destroy demand for products from the United States, China, and other members of the "former EU." In other words, the breakup would not just be loud; it would be long.

If the US dollar strengthens dramatically, US companies would struggle to compete abroad. The United States economy has outperformed much of the rest of the world since the financial crisis. If not in the pace of growth, then certainly in the consistency of growth. This was a tailwind to US companies, who found there domestic economy as a bastion of growth and stability. This may turn into a headwind for US firms as growth shift elsewhere and a stronger dollar makes foreign firms more competitive.

It is worth noting that currency moves tend to "overshoot" and stay there for a long time. It is true that low oil prices are a positive for consumer consumption. But the shift of consumption from gasoline to other items is not a shift to domestic purchases as it once was. Instead, it is a pivot from "drilled in the USA" to goods that may or may not have been made domestically—and probably were not. On the whole, the US manufacturing base is finding itself under competitive threat while losing one of its few promising growth stories in the oil patch.

Drilling is important for the growth of more than a couple states. Colorado, Wyoming, New Mexico, and Arkansas are all heavily reliant on oil to drive their economic growth. It might be difficult to see how the contagion could spread from these relatively small economies. But unforeseen shocks may come from the Southern economies. That region has bolstered US economic statistics for the past decade.

Demographics will not cause a second "Great Recession" in terms of a sharp contraction in economic activity. But an aging population in the United States—and globally—will slow the US growth rate to a crawl. This is almost worse than a recession. At least with a recession there is *typically* a sharp pickup in activity from the bottom. The demographic impact of an aging population is a persistent headwind to growth. One that does not dissipate cyclically in the way many other headwinds would.

This is where the US national debt, and the levels of other developed nations, becomes an issue. Monetary policy is one of the few alternatives left to carry the load of countercyclical economic activism. The amount of debt developed countries currently carry is a severely limiting factor in the ability to counteract downturns. There is some debate about whether the US and others are actually too indebted. The perception is that they are. And perceptions matter. The good news for governments is that pensioners and retirees around the world are financing government borrowing at incredibly low—and sometimes negative—interest rates. Despite low rates, unwillingness or inability to use countercyclical deficit spending can spark unrest in the domestic population. (Greece is a prime example.) And it could create disenfranchisement among the portion of the population taking the brunt of the economic adjustments. Slow growth and lack of political will could contribute to longer (though shallow) recessions and slower, more tepid recoveries.

None of this means there is an imminent collapse of the US economy and other graying societies. But it does imply that "potential" economic growth may be lower. And it will be difficult to jump-start the US growth engine. A recent McKinsey Global Institute piece gave a solution: increasing productivity. In an age where employment is increasingly precious, the global economic landscape is more likely to see increased competition for jobs between nations—not a concentration on increased productivity.

Locating the catalyst for a recession is typically a fools errand. But any of these could metastasize into something that pushes a vulnerable after normal economy into a downturn.

Currency War

But the Fed and the other central banks will save the US economy from the next downturn. Maybe, but maybe not. Instead, it may be all they can do to not be the primary catalyst.

In the after normal, central banks never breached the line of waging a currency war. Their actions, many of which may seem warlike on the surface, arise from far more benign motives. Many central banks have mandated inflation targets either imposed on themselves or through legislation. In most regions, inflation is below target. With a slowing global economy, there had been few ways to keep inflation up to code. But a turn in US monetary policy has made it possible for central banks to meet their policy goals by reflating their domestic economies.

Many of the central banks who have missed their goals are the global economic heavyweights, whose policy shifts have more potent effects on global markets than others. Europe is struggling with stubbornly high unemployment, deflation, and a Greek epic with seemingly no end. Japan has been stagnant for most of the 21st century and faces a truly horrific demographic profile. China is fighting to avoid the side effects associated with rising wages, slowing growth, and increasing deflationary pressures. The central banks of these nations are forced to take actions to thwart domestic economic catastrophes. Often those policies could be construed as currency war-esque. Especially versus the US dollar.

There were few reasons for global central banks to competitively devalue their currencies against the US dollar. After all, the US is the world's buyer of first resort. And with the Federal Reserve "lifting-off" from the its policy of holding rates close to 0% (the "zero lower bound") and continuing to tighten, the US dollar's value rose dramatically. Granted, it has come off its highs, but it remains near them. Instead of waging a currency war, central banks who chose to embark on new or additional QE packages—Japan and the EU—were making legitimate attempts to meet their mandates.

QE tends to increase the prices of domestic investment assets and lower yields on sovereign debt. After all, it is the practice of buying specific assets, pushing prices higher, and forcing investors to find different and new options. Under the US asset purchase program, prices of assets from equities to housing were boosted, inflation was steadily positive, and employment increased. The Fed never quite sustainably reached its target of 2% inflation. Still, the US withstood much of the global deflationary pressure and created jobs. It is reasonable that facing similar circumstances, other central banks would make a similar determination to increase domestic asset prices and loosen financial conditions.

There is another issue at play here—namely, the US dollar had not strengthened significantly in a long time. For the first decade of the 21st century, the US maintained a low exchange rate policy for an extended period of time to enhance economic competitiveness. That is to say, it acted more like a developing country and waged a quiet currency war. The current devaluation of global currencies is less of a currency war and more of a rush to benefit from something much of the world has been waiting for: the revaluation of the US dollar. Now the global economy and the US must come to grips with a dollar revaluation after the US spent the better part of a decade holding down the dollar's value.

In many ways, the US dollar is acting as though it is emerging from a sort of "pegged currency regime." The Fed maintained this "peg" marvelously well too. Even without an explicit mandate or target. Essentially, the Greenspan/Bernanke "*Limbo Peg*" (how low can it go) ensured low interest rates and an active Fed. Now, following an extended period of QE, the Fed has begun to abandon its peg. And central banks around the world do not know how to react. Or how not to react.

No one has declared monetary war. Not so far anyway. But if there is one, China is likely to initiate it. As the US economy was about to hit the Great Recession, many economists were calling for China to revalue the yuan. China was building foreign currency reserves. America's inability to compete was causing many politicians to cry currency manipulation. The weak dollar essentially allowed US jobs to slowly bleed overseas—instead of flood. Now there is an increasing consensus that China will further devalue its currency to spur exports. As became painfully obvious during the summer of 2015, the yuan was—and could be in the future—a source of global financial volatility. Japan is the developed world power that is most likely to retaliate. The currency war would likely remain regional, but other players—namely the ASEAN nations—would be willing combatants.

At the moment, there is no currency war. There is the risk that at some point China devalues suddenly and dramatically and in doing so, spurs a competitive devaluation race in Asia. But the revaluation of the US dollar and central banks acting in their own domestic best interest does not imply something more sinister.

There may have been a few skirmishes. For example, there is a probability that Japan's Halloween 2015 announcement of an easing package was strategically timed for maximum effect. But when central banks have few options to spur inflation and growth, there is a tendency to try things for a short-term gain that have longer-term results. If US monetary policy persistently deviates from the direction of the rest (tightening while others loosen), other monetary authorities will appear hostile with their easing policies.

But the policies are not hostile and have not been hostile. Instead, the world's reserve currency, the US dollar, is reversing years of loose monetary policy, and China, the world's driver of economic growth, is slowing. This forces economies to rethink their growth models. All while attempting to reflate their domestic economies and assets. And from certain angles, this will certainly appear to be a war in the making. Or even one that has already begun. But these actions are the best efforts by institutions under fire to meet policy targets. There may be a currency war coming in the wake of the next downturn, but—for now—the markets are witnessing a violent return to dollar normalcy in a slower inflation and low growth world.

THE CURRENCIES

The Dollar Is a Big Deal

Rumors of the dollar's demise have been greatly exaggerated. Its status as the world's reserve currency is not under siege. In many ways, it is under less pressure than it has been in quite some time. Most recently, the yuan, or renminbi (RMB), has been cited as a possible replacement. Before that, it was the euro threatening to dethrone the dollar. And before the euro, it was the yen. Yet there never seems to be a real, tangible shift in the global trading system, and the dollar remains the world's global reserve currency.

Often, it is tempting for economists to point out intriguing trends and predict the most extreme gloom and doom scenarios. Remember, when the Japanese economy was set to overtake the US? Japan spent the next decade with GDP and price level growth of about 0%. Sometimes it is difficult to articulate a continuation of the status quo.

The data on currency reserves is less than comprehensive. The IMF's Currency Composition of Official Foreign Exchange Reserves (COFER) provides some level of detail but has a number of sources missing. (The report analyzes the currency composition of assets. So a US Treasury bill denominated in dollars counts as dollars). But there are some interesting takeaways from the data. In the first quarter of 2017, the US dollar constitutes 64% of allocated reserves. This is certainly far from its peak of 72% in 2001, but it is similar to the levels seen in the mid-'90s. In other words, the data does not suggest an end to the dollar's run as the predominant reserve currency.

It is worth understanding how the US dollar won the role of reserve currency in the first place. Though the exact timing is debated (and in this debate time is denominated in decades, not years), the best evidence—from Eichengreen and Flandreau—is that the dollar overtook the sterling somewhere in the mid-1920s, lost it briefly, and then regained it in 1929. The Great Depression saw the sterling regain its prominence only to lose its status again to the dollar soon after. France, the China of its day in terms of foreign currency reserves, was largely responsible for tipping the scales toward US dollar dominance.

There is no clean shift from one currency to another. In considering how the dollar's dominance in reserve status may someday evolve toward a more multi-polar reserve currency basket, it is necessary to understand what the shifts look like. Reserve shifts are slow processes, typically accompanied by crises. We might reasonably ask why the Great Recession did not have more of an effect on the dollar's dominance. The simple answer is that—at the moment—there is no viable alternative. The RMB is heavily manipulated. The euro has the (somewhat unreasonable) overhang of its possible dissolution hanging over it. And the yen is impaired by the Bank of Japan's relentless easing program. Granted, the US dollar has not performed ideally for a reserve currency, but no currency ever will.

Economic stability and the ability to hold value are preconditions to seizing and maintaining the mantle of reserve currency. The era of QE could have brought the dollar's durability as a store of value into question. But it did not. The US dollar lost value—but it was never at risk of dissolving. And the only currency with markets liquid enough to challenge the US dollar—the euro—had deep, idiosyncratic issues that threatened its very existence. In essence, there was no alternative to the dollar during the crisis. And there remains no alternative now.

Any potential replacement must have enough debt and a liquid enough market to support it. After all, other countries need to place tremendous amounts of money into the currency. In other words, being a country with a strong economy and stable currency is not enough. It must have deep and reliable debt markets. The euro is the only currency with a market of similar depth to the dollar. China does not have the open system necessary for the RMB to be a reserve currency. It would require significant liberalization of currency movements. It may be able to develop a deep market in RMB. We simply do not know yet. China may be keen to avoid too sharp a slowdown in its own economic growth before putting all the pieces in place to compete as a leading reserve currency.

For the moment, the US dollar looks like a far less risky bet than the currencies bandied about to be its replacement. The euro is inept, and the RMB is incapable of taking the mantle. The dollar will lose its place as the hegemon of currencies at some point, but it should continue to dominate for the foreseeable future.

China Wants In on the Fun

That is not to say that China does not want in on the reserve currency fun. China requested the IMF recommend the RMB as a reserve currency. And Beijing got its wish.

Being a reserve currency economy will eventually give China easier and cheaper access to capital (something an indebted China is in desperate need of at the moment). But there are also drawbacks. Reserve currencies tend to be in high demand, pushing up the value of their currency relative to where it would otherwise trade—something an economy still heavily weighted in exports may not want. A stronger currency makes exports less competitive and imports more competitive. China would not welcome such an outcome. The IMF saying "yes" to the request— and the extent of it (a double digit percent weighting)—has the potential to shift the global economy toward a duopoly with two dominant reserve currencies: the US dollar and the Chinese renminbi. But not any time soon. It will take time and policy shifts for the RMB to gain a weighting even remotely close the US dollar.

The odd thing about the above statement is that the RMB was not considered a reserve currency until the IMF conferred this honor by adding the renminbi to its Special Drawing Right (SDR). The SDR is a sort of IMF reserve currency consisting of specific allocations of stable, global currencies. It is a guide to what global central banks should hold for reserves. Prior to the RMB's inclusion, this was the yen, euro, pound sterling, and US dollar. Regardless of the near-term issues, the RMB is likely to increase its weighting further at some point.

From China's perspective, there is a certain level of prestige that comes with being added to the SDRs. It elevated the RMB to reserve currency status and gave it a recommended holding size for central banks. This is only the first piece of a much larger puzzle around the RMB and reserve-currency status. However, an almost 11% weighting in the SDR places the RMB ahead of the yen weighting, but only a fourth of the weighting given to the US dollar.

Recently, China has been at the center of two new institutions with global aspirations: the so-called "BRICS" bank and the Asian Infrastructure and Investment Bank (AIIB). These institutions could and maybe should be considered counterpoints to similar Western establishments such as the IMF itself or the World Bank. Infrastructure is needed in much of still emerging Asia, and—by providing the funding and framework to construct it—China makes steady strides toward achieving economic and political duopoly status with the United States.

These new institutions are important, not only for their potential influence on development in emerging Asian economies, but for the internationalization of the renminbi. With the RMB approved as a reserve currency, the emerging world may seize this as a chance to use it in trade with their primary trading partners. For many countries that rely on commodity exports to China, it makes sense to trade using RMB. Not to mention, the aforementioned new development institutions may well function with a heavy dose of RMB—if not primarily. This allows the RMB to more easily become the reserve currency of the Southeast Asian region. That would make the transition to becoming a significant global reserve currency much easier.

China is simply following the US playbook, and the legitimacy of these institutions should not be simply thrown aside. China has spent the past decade bringing its infrastructure up to par. It knows how to execute this type of infrastructure based growth model—something Western powers cannot bring to the table. The AIIB is a China-led institution with Chinese goals at its forefront. This constitutes a significant deviation from the current Western-oriented Bretton Woods based model that has dominated global economic influence in the postwar era.

But China's destiny is not solely in its own hands. The potential impact of a euro currency collapse or return to crisis mode should not be underestimated. (Or overestimated for that matter.) In the near term, the financial destruction of China's largest trading partner—Europe—would be difficult to overcome without significant economic consequences. But it would also force central banks to rethink their reserve currency allocations and therefore their long-term economic alignments. If Europe and the monetary union begin to implode, China and the RMB could emerge as the primary beneficiaries of the carnage in the end.

There are reasons to believe that the RMB would gain share even without an implosion of the euro. Central banks appreciate stability. Relatively speaking, China may actually provide the stability they crave. China also has the highest yields—meaning the currency could be attractive to hold. Critically, the US dollar does not have to lose any share of its central bank reserves for the renminbi to become a significant factor.

As mentioned above, the US dollar comprises 64% of allocated global reserves. The euro is a bit above 19%. The latest SDR basket has the US dollar far lower than that figure (42%) and the euro far higher (31%). This is where the opening lies for a viable secondary or tertiary candidate. The euro is the second largest reserve holding, and over time a higher RMB allocation would likely come at the expense of the euro and yen. Not because the US dollar is untouchable, but because it remains the primary currency involved in settling global trade.

The spillover from adding the RMB to the SDR has the potential to accelerate the shift to a truly bipolar—or at least a multi-polar—economic regime. A regimes in which the United States is likely to still dominate—but with fewer and fewer advantages over rivals. If the RMB bursts onto the international scene, it has the potential to cause a sharp transition between currency regimes. This type of violent, unexpected transition risks sparking a crisis in the short term, though little of the longer-run story would be altered.

If all goes smoothly for China, central banks will spend the next decade or so trading euros and yen for RMB. Economic hegemony has already given way, regardless of the IMF's decision. Influence has pivoted to Asia. And it will continue to do so. There are no givens in economics or politics, but it appears that China and the US are on course to an economic and political duopoly with all the benefits and perils that come with it.

The Dollar Should Encourage Other Reserve Currencies

With the arrival of the renminbi in the SDR basket, the Chinese currency has a bit more clout than it did previously. This has caused much rancor among those who believe the dollar should be the sacrosanct leader of the financial world. However, the strength of the dollar clearly slowed the US economy and limited its policy options. The dollar's dominance may be the dollar's problem.

The Fed has struggled with fits and starts to normalize its policy instruments while avoiding the possibility of recession. Much of this pressure could be eased—transferred elsewhere—by encouraging the world's central banks to adopt other currencies as partial replacements to the dollar. The most obvious candidate to spark this movement is the RMB. It is time to let someone else have the burden, and, yes, some of the rewards of being a dominant reserve currency.

Why would the United States even consider sharing its beloved reserve currency status? For starters, it already does. The dollar is dominant, but it is not the sole currency being held by other central banks. The dollar dominates the others in holding size, but dollars, yen, pounds, and euros are all held by central banks in differing amounts and according to the individual needs of differing central banks.

US monetary policy can wreak havoc on other countries' economies with rapid appreciation and depreciation of their currencies. This limits the ability of the Fed to act solely in the best interest of the United States. This is probably the most critical element of being the dominant reserve currency, a reduction in the independence and effectiveness of monetary policy.

To ease pressure on the dollar, the Treasury Department—officially in charge of dollar policy—could pursue a policy of loosening the dollar's dominance of reserve stockpiles and encouraging the diversification of reserves away from the dollar. Instead of pursuing a 21st century Plaza Accord, the US should encourage a strategy of diversification (the Plaza Accord was an agreement in 1985 among major global economic powers to lower the value of the dollar). One example would be asking the IMF to suggest that there be a cap on US dollar denominated reserves—call it 50%. If so, central banks would be sellers of the dollar, pushing it down.

There are a couple reasons this is an attractive option for the United States. The dollar would still be a dominant currency. But the selling pressure on the dollar generated by the other central banks would allow the US to normalize monetary policy more easily and without having a surging dollar choke the American economy. The US would also have room for easy monetary policy without causing issues for the rest of the world. The reduction of the dollar would also allow for deeper integration of other, emerging countries—such as China—into the global financial system. Inclusion of the RMB in the SDR was a start. Increasing its usage may be a benefit to the Western powers. Especially if the usage is within their system.

Previous predictions of the dollar's demise were inevitably wrong. The Japanese economy stalled. The euro ran into problems. And the renminbi does not have the financial infrastructure and markets to back it up. The dollar continues to dominate. The US dollar, always doubted and presumed past its prime, seems to come out of crises unscathed—even stronger.

The dollar's survival is, in part, due to its centrality in the current global economic system. Reasons for this range from historical reasons to a lack of an alternative. But the costs and benefits of the dollar's preeminence are rarely debated. America's economic dominance and Cold War geopolitics required the dollar's dominance. But that need is waning. Regardless, there continues to be a sentiment, especially in the United States, that the dollar's status is needed for the survival of the republic. But there will be little lost if and when the dollar's share in global reserves declines. What is being suggested here is that central banks are likely to benefit from becoming less dollarized—less exposed to a single currency.

There are certainly drawbacks. Politically, the ability to maneuver and manipulate foes or dissenters using the dollarized world would be diminished. Sanctions—such as those currently imposed on Russia—would become harder to pursue. Also of potential concern would be a reduction in the ability to finance deficit spending. In an era of QE and creative monetary policy, however, this fear is far less relevant than it once was.

Ian Bremmer calls this a world suffering from "G-zero" leadership. The world is already politically multipolar with China, the EU, and the US dominating their regions, but has little leadership on a global scale. China has pursued a strategy of creating institutions that rival the Western ones. Meanwhile, trade treaties between the United States and countries on both sides of the Atlantic have faced hurdles at home that have caused them to be canceled outright or caused their passage to be questionable at best.

Without more substantive action, Washington may be losing its ability to make the transition from a unipolar reserve currency system in a less disruptive fashion. And it makes little sense for an increasingly regionalized world to be dominated by dollars. At more than half of global reserves, the dollar is well ahead of all others. But at some point, there will be a reversal—or at least a drawdown—of the overweight positions. The yuan is unlikely to supplant the US dollar any time soon. But it is difficult to find a better time for this shift to occur than when the dollar is strong relative to other currencies. This is unlikely to happen with any rapidity. The dollar has steadfastly held its position of reserve dominance, even as the United States has waned in relative political and economic importance globally.

The Making of After Normal

The Consequence: The End of the Dual Stimuli

The beginning of the 21st century global economy was driven by the US-China relationship. These two countries each contributed stimulus to economic growth. This is the "dual stimuli." Alan Greenspan's perpetually low interest rates allowed the US consumer to splurge on housing. This drove home prices higher. This increase in equity either was directly tapped for consumer purchases or gave the confidence to spend. The housing boom and the demand for new housing compensated for manufacturing and lower skilled jobs that went to China, as construction employment absorbed some of the losses. Still, the employment losses brought stagnant wages, low inflation, and a Fed willing to fight them with persistent stimulus.

And this is how a US generated stimulus built much of China. As low cost manufacturing pivoted to China, Beijing rapidly built the infrastructure necessary to keep pace with ever increasing demand. But now the sustainability of China's economic model of hyper-investment and low cost labor is fading.

The China stimulus—its unprecedented infrastructure boom—drove the commodity producing countries of the world to build capacity as though Chinese demand was going to continue to grow far into the future. For a while, it did. Now with China's domestic infrastructure surge peaking, if not winding down, there are few outlets for the oversupply of commodities and little chance to replace the demand in the near term. The commodity producing nations of the world can look longingly at the Chinese "One Belt, One Road" (OBOR) initiative as a possible future savior. But OBOR is unlikely to save them from their glut.

The world did not lose only the US' QE. It also lost China's commodity boom. This was the beginning of the dual taper. The US and China were no longer going to stimulate the world. And there are dramatic and prolonged consequences for the growth of the global economy. In many ways, the dual taper is indicative of the perils of the after normal economy. The two largest economies in the world ramped their stimulus then wound them down, and the entire world felt the repercussions.

The Dual Taper

Having built a $4 plus trillion balance sheet, the Fed is slowly raising interest rates. The timing and velocity at which interest rates will be hiked is not firm and has waxed and waned during the tightening years. Even the extent to which they are willing to maintain the size of the balance sheet over the long run is unclear. But it is evident that the Fed would like for there to be a semblance of normalcy in policy again one day. The consequence? After years of artificially weak exchange rates, the US dollar surged to decade highs, causing its own fallout.

Meanwhile, China and its two decade long boom are on tenuous ground. China is shifting to a consumer model and away from an investment and infrastructure growth model. Many countries have built their growth models on China, and now the validity and longevity of those models are being challenged. The combination of plentiful dollars and insatiable demand for infrastructure had been powerful stimuli for the global economy. But the dual taper is well under way, and the effects could continue to be violent and cause prolonged volatility in the global economy.

The dual stimuli is not a recent phenomenon. This helps explain how the global economy became addicted to it. The emergence of the dual stimuli occurred somewhere around the start of the 21st century—as Chinese growth began to surge and interest rates in the US approached zero. The Federal Reserve under Alan Greenspan rode loose US monetary policy for the better part of the pre-crisis 21st century, something he himself called "extraordinary." The Greenspan Fed did this for legitimate reasons, as the global competition for jobs and rising levels of inequality at home spurred increasing levels of concern. American manufacturing jobs were being relocated to China. Greenspan's time at the Fed saw this trend accelerate and become difficult to ignore.

In shepherding the American stimulus, Greenspan seems to have seen the growing pressure on American workers' wages and the emerging global contestability of jobs. In February 2005, Greenspan laid out his thoughts:

> Technological advance is continually altering the shape, nature, and complexity of our economic processes. But technology and, more recently, competition from abroad have grown to a point at which demand for the least-skilled workers in the United States and other developed countries is diminishing, placing downward pressure on their wages. These workers will need to acquire the skills required to compete effectively for the new jobs that our economy will create.

Greenspan knew he was fighting an uphill battle against engrained, secular forces. But these headwinds also allowed—forced even—the Fed to maintain low interest rates without the typical side effects of inflation (except in housing). There would be consequences from prolonged low rates, but runaway inflation would not be one of them.

Greenspan was not incorrect either. Blue collar employment losses kept inflation tame in the early 2000s—through a lack of wage inflation to the middle skilled workforce. The Fed, seeing little inflation and an unusual jobs picture, kept interest rates abnormally low for an abnormally long time (or so it seemed at the time) to spur job creation and spark some wage inflation. History is still judging this episode (and it is unlikely to be kind), but those passing out judgment tend to miss the logic of the thinking. If carefully considered, it makes sense in retrospect.

Without those low rates, it may have been obvious earlier that the US was struggling with the growing symptoms of secular stagnation—or at least flirting with it. After all, the Fed was allowing a housing bubble to form to create the type of jobs impossible to find in other sectors of the economy—low to non-contestable ones. Construction jobs were easy transitions from the manufacturing floor, and they are not easily taken offshore or automated. Housing and the construction jobs it brought were a sort of counterpoint to China's manufacturing employment gains from the US.

How did this inter-occupational jobs transfer play out? Construction was spurred by a more than doubling of mortgage debt between 2000 and 2008, and consumers leveraged their balance sheets with all kinds of credit. The Fed kept the debt cheap, adding fuel to the housing and consumer boom, particularly after the Nasdaq bubble burst and September 11 pulled the US back to the Middle East.

But Greenspan was not just overheating the US housing market. To keep pace with the demand for cheap goods, China was driven to build its infrastructure rapidly as demand for its exports rose—especially from the credit fueled US. Since 2000, US demand for China's goods has increased nearly fourfold. It may have appeared a US housing bubble had few (or no) implications for China. But it was US demand—for cheap goods and labor—that spurred much of the infrastructure building. Greenspan, attempting to spur employment in America, built China.

China Builds Everything

Construction in China was measured in cities per year, and most important, China imported these cities. From iron ore and copper to the energy used to power the new cities, the inputs were and are largely brought in from other countries. On the other side of the equation, consumption by American consumers was a constantly increasing function of their willingness to take on more debt. Then the US growth stopped and imports from China declined. In what proved to be a successful effort to ward off the effects of the Great Recession, China embarked on an aggressive infrastructure stimulus.

Prior to the Great Recession, China was already building—at an unfathomable pace. The stimulus further accelerated this investment. This spending spurred on China's own economy. It also stimulated the economies of its commodity exporting trading partners. Australia alone saw an increase of A$10 billion in exports to China in 2009. Thanks to Chinese commodity demand, Australia slowed only modestly, actually growing its economy through the Great Recession.

But it is not a free ride for Australia, and there are drawbacks. One of which is that any sharp Chinese slowdown would send demand for Australian raw materials plummeting. And Australia is not the only country. The effects would be felt much more widely. Many emerging market economies exploited and relied heavily on their resource industries to piggyback China's rise. A change in China's growth patterns has proven ruinous to some of their economies. The "RIBS"—Russia, India, Brazil, and South Africa—largely rely on commodities to drive their economies, with the obvious exception of India. The rest are finding it difficult to adapt to the post China boom though. Brazil now finds itself in the midst of a recession. And Russia is facing the fallout of the collapse in oil prices. Even without a crisis or the dreaded hard landing, a slowdown in China has exposed the hyper-over-investment the world engaged in to support China's growth. A marginal slowdown has meant marginal projects became unprofitable quickly.

There are a few reasons to fret about China's economic health. China is shifting from a production oriented model to a consumption model, but it cannot simply leave its export manufacturing and investment model behind. It is not a painless transition. According to the Boston Consulting Group, due to stagnant wage growth, the US and a rejuvenated Mexico are becoming increasingly competitive with China. Instead of the tailwind of stagnant wages in the developed world, wages are rising in China. This means that pressures are intensifying on China's manufacturing sector as the transition continues. Infrastructure investment is unlikely to be the easy answer it once was to China, though the government continues to pursue this as a method of smoothing growth. The economy must pivot. But this is not easy—as Greenspan would attest to. It costs jobs in fields where prospects of transition to a new occupation are bleak. Maintaining previous wage levels are even bleaker. Unfortunately, China's transition will continue to cause the global economy to be more volatile.

The Beneficiaries

China's stimulus drove growth in countless emerging economies, where (typically extractive oriented) infrastructure was constructed to support China's infrastructure building. But Fed policy, the other tailwind for commodity producers, cannot be ignored. Commodity producers benefitted from a weak US dollar as the Fed first held interest rates low and then experimented with unconventional tactics. A weak dollar commands a lower price for commodities in non-dollar terms. This stimulates demand. For the last decade, then, the US has been stimulating demand for commodities worldwide in an attempt to spur on its own domestic growth.

In other words, China's infrastructure boom supported global volume, while low rates followed by QE put a floor under demand and prices by pressuring the US dollar lower. Commodity producers had the best of both worlds: China and the US both working at the same time to hold the commodity bubble together. They may soon see the worst of all possible worlds.

Australia is a case study in overshooting the China story with at least one commodity: coal. In recent years, Australia built coal mine after coal mine to satiate China's steel industry and electric utilities. The bet paid off. At least for a few years. But then came the oversupply and declining prices. Mines have already been shuttered. Further signs of China slowing would portend more closures. This is particularly distressing for Australia, with coal being its second largest export behind iron ore. China has become the destination for over 28% of Australia's exports in 2016 and since the turn of the century, constitutes nearly half the growth in exports.

And the type of commodity matters. There is a difference between commodities used for consumption and those used for infrastructure. A commodity used for consumption would be less impacted by a slowdown in investment. The end use of coal differs from the iron ore and copper used in infrastructure. Global iron ore demand is dominated by China, which constitutes approximately half of it. But after rising consistently, iron ore prices have fallen to post-recession lows and have not recovered to nearly its mid-stimulus highs. This is not only a product of Chinese demand but also of an incredible amount of supply brought on to support the demand, creating a surplus. The story of copper is similar—except that copper demand would have been negative without the marginal demand from China over the past decade. As China steps back, the commodity demand glut is in a perilous position. Even Chinese authorities have expressed a desire to cut China's surplus steel production capacity.

But there is more to the story. Australia and Canada have strong ties to China's infrastructure. They also boast two of the hottest housing markets in the developed world. Canada's economy entirely avoided the financial crisis, and Australia's housing prices have marched steadily higher. Much of their success during and following the financial crisis should be directly attributed to their economies relying so heavily on commodities and the Chinese infrastructure stimulus. Not to mention the incremental benefit of creating jobs in constructing the facilities needed to meet the projected increase in demand. But it now seems unlikely all of the anticipated demand will ever materialize. And neither economy reset their financial system during the Great Recession as the US was forced to do. This leaves the commodity countries—not simply Canada and Australia—vulnerable to a decline in the volume of commodity exports and further, to generally lower prices. Lower prices lead to right sizing of supply, the shuttering of high cost mines, and the loss of employment. And lower employment leads to lower consumption and so on.

Australia and Canada (also read Chile, Peru, Brazil, New Zealand, and South Africa) have benefited from employment and economic activity that makes economic sense only at elevated commodity prices. Mining companies tend to finance construction with high debt loads. If China scales back its commodity appetite, some of this debt begins to sour. For Canada and Australia, a rapid collapse in the demand, and therefore price and volumes, of commodities could spell trouble for their housing markets. The Great Recession was sparked by tenuous and illiquid financial assets in the US. Those countries tied to China face the prospect of something similar.

Australia and Canada are far more leveraged than even the worst European nations. In fact, there are relatively few countries in which households have continued to leverage themselves in recent years. Even the infamously irresponsible economies of Southern Europe have slowly deleveraged. And this is where the true danger lies. The leverage to the continuation of the commodity boom is not simply a theoretical abstract that could damage their GDP numbers. The slowdown is already having a pronounced effect on both Australia and Canada. It is no coincidence that they are also two of the countries that rely most heavily, in terms of GDP and export contribution, on mining. About 5% of Australia's GDP, and nearly 40% of its exports, is related to mining. Canada is similar, with around 4% of GDP and 30% of exports. The relatively small contributions to GDP hide the secondary industrial ties to commodity extraction and exportation: transportation, the construction of the infrastructure to handle the raw materials, machinery, and so forth. Canada may have some cushion given its exposure to the US, but the US has its own energy renaissance under way and may not be the demand stabilizer it once was.

For Australia and Canada, the result is that the roll-off of the Chinese stimulus has the potential to be slowly devastating. Now, though, there is an increasing likelihood that consequences could work through their financial systems, with wages and employment adjusting to lower volumes and prices of commodities. This in turn reduces the ability of households in these markets to consume and leverage. Housing prices will likely fall, reducing implicit savings and net worth. This further reduces the ability to consume. In essence, the leverage to the commodity boom has the potential to turn commodity deflation into real economy deflation and stagnation. Not a pleasant outcome.

The US Makes It Worse

US monetary policy heightens the problems faced by the commodity producers as well. Instead of a single headwind, they are dealing with the end of the dual stimuli. Excessive Chinese demand is fading, and a stronger US dollar damages pricing and trade further. Globally, no country is able to step in to replace Chinese demand. Europe and Japan will continue to stimulate their economies, but this will serve only to further strengthen the dollar. And the negative feedback loop continues.

Now, Janet Yellen would like to maintain a neutral monetary policy to ward off inequality and the contestability of US employment. As the dual stimuli comes to an end, contestability is an issue the Fed should be fretting about with America's own commodity linkages. Yellen's statements in October 2014 on inequality at a Boston Federal Reserve Conference on Economic Opportunity and Inequality drew criticism, but her comments were directly connected to ensuring the US has created enough *uncontestable* jobs for the Fed sustainably to step away from its accommodative policy stance, which it has begun to do. These jobs are the type that could lead to the upward wage pressures that have yet to take hold in the recovery. Housing construction created the uncontestable jobs during the last recovery. Until the oil price bust, the shale oil boom was creating them this time around. While intended to reflate asset prices and spur inflation and employment, QE also had a significant effect on the price of commodities.

As mentioned before, Raghuram Rajan, the head of the Reserve Bank of India, stated in an April 2014 address at the Brookings Institution that "some advanced economy central bankers have privately expressed their worry that the QE 'works' primarily by altering exchange rates…." In other words, without the effect that QE has on exchange rates—lower for the US dollar when the Fed engages in it—there may not be much of an effect at all. It is also likely that the highly accommodative Fed policy resulted in a dollar that was weaker than it otherwise would have been. And this is the main mechanism through which QE is transmitted to global markets. The depreciating dollar leads to commodities that are more expensive in dollar terms. Rajan was making a claim that is far more significant than it initially appears.

And this was a boost to the US economy. In fact, the US was a prime example of the power the dual stimuli had on commodity markets and economies. Higher oil prices made more US shale production possible, and therefore more hiring in the oil sector, and more marginal projects to be profitable. Oil was central to the US recovery story, and oil patch jobs mattered. After all, Texas contributed 32% of US GDP growth between 2007 and 2013. One reason that oil patch jobs are so critical is the general requirement of the presence of the worker and that most jobs cannot be done without a significant amount of education. The "presence of the worker" requirement makes them impossible to offshore or relocate—many of the oil field jobs are *uncontestable*.

Now, with QE completed and the global supply imbalances, the US shale revolution is being pressured, and in some areas, at least temporarily shuttered. Projects were undertaken that made sense only at higher prices, and capital budgets are being slashed as prices remain depressed. Granted, this is not a perfect example, but it illustrates the effects of oversupply and a strong dollar.

The Fed should have watched this closely. The United States actually relied on oil for a significant portion of its high quality employment growth after the Great Recession. Sustained lower prices could spell long-term trouble for a bright spot in the US economy.

The Weakest Link

Commodities are the weakest link between the two stimuli. China and the US used unique mechanisms of intervening to spur growth. But they ultimately affected the commodity markets by pushing prices and volumes above a globally sustainable level. It is too late to make better capital allocations with those stimuli. And much of the capital spending—tied to marginal commodity extraction—could become a transmission mechanism of the next shock. Households in much of the emerging world never delevered during the Great Recession, because there was no reason to do so.

How will the world react when there is nothing propping it up? Can stimulus packages from the ECB and Bank of Japan (BoJ) make up for the conclusion of the "great dual stimuli"? Probably not. All it takes is a slowdown, a slight step back by China, and a lack of monetary stimulus from the Fed for commodities to continue their malaise. The economic pivot in China requires a global economic transition. Changing will be difficult for China to execute. The rest of world is also not prepared to deal with the new reality. The dollar has already risen to levels not seen in a decade. There are few signs it will weaken back toward the lows of the QE era any time soon. Without the dual stimuli, the global economy is being forced to rebalance. But it is simply not prepared to deal with the consequences.

Nothing Left to Lose?

Likely due to the slowdown of global growth following the conclusion of the dual stimuli, Fed Chair Janet Yellen has found herself at various points during her tenure defending the independence of the institution in charge of setting the nation's monetary policy. The pressure on the Fed, while not a new phenomenon (Rand Paul has been suggesting the Fed be looked at for a while), seems to be building.

Suggestions for how to control the Fed range from the adoption of a specific rule to guide policy to an external review of Fed decisions. The problem? None of these will cause policy outcomes to be any better than they are now. Monetary policy running at the speed of Congress is a deeply disturbing thought. In the context of having politicians involved in the monetary policy apparatus, political gridlock could do real, tangible harm to the US economy.

Political interference is inevitable. After all, monetary policy can be a powerful political tool. And there are good reasons for lawmakers to pressure for oversight now. Many observers—not only economists—see the Fed's actions in the early days of the Great Recession as having staved off something potentially far more vicious. Meanwhile, the recovery suffered from prolonged periods of countercyclical cuts in government spending that the Fed was forced to ease policy through.

Congress already has fiscal policy at its discretion, and fiscal spending is a powerful tool. Fiscal stimulus—cutting taxes and increasing spending on infrastructure—provides a powerful boost directly to constituent income statements. Meanwhile, monetary policy can affect balance sheets by causing asset prices to move higher. There are reasons these two policies are separately determined. The combination of the two is powerful and may be too tempting to deploy in too many circumstances. Now, they are determined separately in the United States (and most developed countries). Monetary policy rests with the Fed and fiscal policy with Congress. It should stay that way.

After the Great Recession, there were calls for more coordinated action on the part of fiscal and monetary policy to accomplish goals more quickly in the wake of, or during, crises. The independence of fiscal and monetary policies from one another allows them to intentionally act in concert or not. For example, the Federal Reserve decides to lower interest rates and Congress passes a stimulus bill. The two are acting independently but in concert. Furthermore, two independent bodies are required to interpret the current, and future, economic situation and whether stimulus is needed—a sort of economic system of checks and balances.

Economic cycles do not and should not coincide with political cycles. Take the case of the Central Bank of the Republic of Turkey (CBRT). It is by law an independent institution. But it does not appear as though the CBRT is functionally independent. Turkish President Recep Tayyip Erdogan once stated that supporting high interest rates is treasonous. Erdogan persistently called for lower interest rates. The CBRT obliged, though not as aggressively as the president would have preferred.

It is unlikely the Fed will experience outright threats or calls of tyranny. Any hint of political maneuvering through Fed policy would be skewered by the media, and it is unlikely individual views on interest rate direction or levels will ever be considered treasonous. But there are reasons politicians cannot resist pushing for oversight or exerting soft power on the monetary authority. The tools that central bankers wield are powerful and therefore attractive to those who want power.

Turkey is not the only country with a central bank being twisted from its purpose. Becoming part of the Troika and overseeing the Greek bailout blurred the nature of the ECB. Instead of providing stability in times of economic strife, the ECB became a political tool and source of volatility and instability. (Imagine the Fed monitoring a bailout of Illinois.) As mentioned, the threat of being cut off from ECB lifelines may deter Greek officials from pushing the limits of their bailout package. But it may also cause Greeks to stop looking at the ECB as a backstop and more like a German weapon to impose and perpetuate austerity. The ECB shifted from being politicized to weaponized

Yellen's fear should be that the Fed will become too much like the ECB was or the CBRT is. Both institutions are heavily politicized and far less effective in achieving their policy goals than the Fed. In many ways, the Fed may be a victim of its own under-politicization. Under previous chairs, the United States maintained a low exchange rate for an extended period of time to enhance economic competitiveness and keep or create jobs that would not otherwise exist. In essence, it acted like a central bank that was politicized. Yellen should continue to fight the calls for congressional oversight and second guessing—not because Fed decisions are without flaw, but because mixing politicians with monetary policy would create far worse outcomes.

Attempting the Yellen Accord

The Plaza Accord was a truly coordinated effort by the G5 economic powers to spur economic growth. In 1985, the finance ministers of France, West Germany, Japan, the United States, and the United Kingdom met, and agreed to lower the value of the US dollar. Although the goal was explicit, it was also vague: "Devalue the dollar." Recently, central banks coordinated their policy decisions again. Instead of summits and meetings between finance ministers, central banks have a new method to conduct their policy coordination: transparency. Policy transparency from the Fed allows other central banks to anticipate its policy actions—for better or worse—and respond accordingly. This is the Yellen Accord—and it may have saved the European economy.

The Yellen Accord was a much subtler construct than the Plaza Accord, but it appears to have been nearly as successful as its predecessor. This time, to spur economic growth, the major central banks forced a revaluation of the dollar—whether the Fed liked it or not. The impact, both near and far, should not be discounted. The dollar appreciated substantially. And this decision was not made by the Federal Reserve or the US Treasury.

To set the stage, the eurozone economy needed to avoid a triple dip recession, and the US economy had stimulated its way out of a recession. The Fed eliminated bond purchases (QE) and intimated that there would be interest rate increases (though not immediately or quickly). By thus tightening monetary policy (or removing accommodation) ever so slightly, Chair Yellen did precisely what should be done by a relatively strong economy. Meanwhile, the ECB took a reasonable course of action by launching a bond buying program. By explicitly stating their policy intentions and direction, the Fed tacitly allowed the ECB and the BoJ to time their decisions optimally around the Fed's and achieve their mandates.

The eurozone was in need of this type of intervention. The United States also needs to be able to survive it. A dramatically weaker euro and stronger dollar could have caused problems for the US economy. Without the Fed's relative policy tightness, Draghi's stimulus program would not have been as successful at weakening the euro. US monetary policy is part of the current ECB stimulus package. A deviation from the current path of tightening by the Fed threatens to knock the Draghi stimulus—and therefore a European recovery—off course.

On its own, the ECB probably does not have the policy firepower it needs to spark the desired inflation and employment outcome in the eurozone. Luckily for the ECB, the Yellen Accord transparency provides ways to achieve outcomes that would not be possible for central banks without it. The shift toward openness by the global central banks has fundamentally changed the policy options available to central banks. Fed policy may not aim to accomplish objectives beyond its border, but it is certainly not blocking them.

Yellen and the Fed essentially allowed for the euro and yen to rebalance in a similar fashion to previously coordinated efforts. To a degree, forward guidance and openness are simpler methods of coordinating policy actions between central banks—for better or worse. The need for credibility makes it far more difficult for a central bank to break from a stated path. When the Fed has guided markets toward a certain policy stance or outcome, any surprise deviations damage the credibility of the institution. And lack of credibility is something to be feared by a monetary authority.

Policy coordination is largely mechanical in nature—selling or buying currencies and raising or lowering interest rates. But transparency of policy movements and regimes removes the need to overtly coordinate and articulate. Such openness removes the pain point of coordination, but it could also lead to cheating and "overshooting." In other words, piggybacking on the Fed's policy shift works until someone begins to take advantage of the situation beyond the reasonable. (This is why—in the era of transparency—it is all the more crucial to keep the central bank separate from the central government.)

This policy is unlikely to produce all benefits and no costs. The Plaza Accord was not beneficial to all parties involved and took a considerable toll on some. The mission of devaluing the US dollar was successful, but the Plaza Accord was painful for the Japanese economy. The yen rose dramatically as the Accord was implemented. This prompted stimulus measures to offset the appreciation. And that fostered an asset bubble, which burst, necessitating a decade of recovery.

Now the Yellen Accord has taken its toll on the dollar. The revaluation appears to have been orderly thus far. But there may still be pain to come, as the world economy grapples with something it has not seen in a long time: a strong dollar. Coordinating policy had been out of vogue for a quarter century. But central banks have quietly brought it back. The Fed and its global counterparts have entered a new era of central banking. One in which a loose form of policy coordination is the new normal and the ability of central banks to address—as well as cause—economic problems is amplified.

For now, it means the BoJ and ECB are magnifying the movements of the Fed. Yellen is well aware of the risks of this policy. Someone could take the Yellen Accord for granted and (over) shoot the global economy in the foot.

The Debt Limit: One Reason the Fed Can't Let Interest Rates Go Too High

While the Yellen Accord unfolds, it is worth remembering that one of the principle reasons that the US federal government's debt is affordable is the current low interest rate environment. Currently, there is an unprecedented amount of debt, but the level of US debt could be either safely contained or mortally high. It depends on when, if, and by how much interest rates rise in the future. Not the rates the Fed controls, but the long-term interest rates on government debt. Even while the Fed has been raising the fed funds rate, these longer-term rates have moved little or even fallen. We know neither the timing nor the extent interest rates will rise in the future—not to mention the level of debt that will need to be refinanced. This means that the debt situation is in a sort of limbo. We simply do not know when, or if, it will explode.

There are certainly reasons to be concerned. The absolute amount of debt amassed by the federal government is at an unprecedented $20 trillion with $14 trillion held by the public, about 104% of GDP. These are astounding amounts. But the level of debt is not the end of the story. The level of debt does not determine the amount of interest expense tied to the accumulated debt.

Debt to GDP is an often cited metric. It is catchy, simple to use and calculate, and sounds ominous. (A 100% debt to GDP really means that if all of GDP were used to repay debt, it would take one year to do it.) But it is a deficient measure. GDP itself cannot be used to repay the national debt, and then there is the question of real or nominal GDP use. GDP is a measure of consumption but also contains government spending, inventories, and transfer payments—none of which should be counted in a metric that is attempting to convey information about a country's indebtedness or ability to repay.

A far more relevant figure would be the amount of revenue the government is receiving—its tax receipts. GDP does not provide an indication of future government revenues or even potential government revenues. Stepping back for a minute, we should remember that other countries have spent decades far above the 100% debt-to-GDP ratio (Japan, for instance) without imploding, though not thriving either. Much the same criticism could be levied against the overuse of the "debt" number. The amount of debt is (to an extent) irrelevant—so long as the interest payments are manageable.

A more relevant and simple way to evaluate the seriousness of a country's debt addiction is comparing a government's revenues to the interest expense of its debt—"payments to revenue." Simply, how much does the government collect during a fiscal year, how much does the government spend on interest in a fiscal year, and how does this compare to history?

This gives a useful indication of the actual cost of debt accumulation—not simply the size of the stockpile. It also provides a more complete context to the evolution of the federal debt by implicitly including interest rates and any changes that might be made to the tax code. Changes to the tax code would influence the "revenue" denominator, and higher interest rates would cause the "payments" numerator to grow.

Using this measurement, America's federal debt picture brightens significantly. Whereas debt to GDP is 104% and has persistently crept higher, the ratio of payments to revenue has consistently moved lower. The total debt outstanding is sitting at an all-time high at more than $20T. Still, both net interest expense and total interest expense are off their highs. (Net interest subtracts the payments on the roughly $5.5 trillion in intragovernmental debt holdings from the total interest payment.)

For perspective, the Office of Management and Budget historical tables reveal that the net interest payment in 1995 was $232 billion or 17% of government revenues. In 2015, the net interest payment was $223 billion or about 7% of revenues. Despite the ominous debt-to-GDP headlines, net interest payment amount in 2015 was roughly the same as 20 years prior. And the net interest payments are consuming less than half the budget space.

Granted, the Federal Reserve's low interest rate policy and subsequent QE program has caused borrowing rates to decline to historically low levels. The aforementioned decline of interest payments to revenues was due to interest rates declining over the past couple decades. But not as low as the negative rates currently seen in Japan and Europe. Therefore, the Fed is principally responsible for the phenomenon of the low interest expenses on government debt. Some credit for the better economy and increasing revenue should be given to the Fed for its monetary intervention.

But there are still some worries. The potential for interest rates to rise in the future poses the most danger. There is a much higher debt level now but a lower cost of debt service to revenues. There is no denying the debt amassed by the US federal government is considerable and has the potential to cause problems down the road. But looking at the issue through the narrow lens of debt to GDP would be a fallacy. Well publicized papers have argued that beyond a certain debt-to-GDP level, economic growth slows. In reality, the slowing was probably more attributable to changes in the costs of servicing that debt. The economics of debt changes as do the situations and context.

The US "debt problem" is either nearing a crisis point (as it careens over the "slow growth" threshold) or is in fine shape because revenue increases have outstripped interest payments. At the moment, there are plenty of revenues to cover the interest expenses, regardless of the absolute level of debt. The US economy has dealt with higher revenue to interest paid before.

This Keeps the Fed Stuck in Neutral

Luckily for the constant debate on the national debt (as evidenced by debt ceiling debates happening too frequently), interest rates are unlikely to be going too high too soon. There is always an ideal level of interest rates. According to the Fed, the ideal is the neutral (or natural or equilibrium) rate of interest at the moment. The neutral interest rate can be defined as the fed funds rate consistent with an economy operating at its "potential" with Fed policy acting to accelerate or decelerate the growth rate. And this—somewhat odd—economic guide may become an increasingly important data point for those watching the Fed's policies closely over the next few years.

Estimates suggest the policy neutral rate has been declining since the 1960s (with a slight uptick during the booming 1990s). An accurate tagline might be "Still Stuck in Neutral." One major bond house recently called this "The New Neutral." But a declining neutral rate is anything but new.

The neutral rate is a long-term indicator that is slow to change. It can be affected by the same demographic and technological trends that affect the broader economy—including debt levels. A simple way to think about the neutral policy rate is as the sum of potential GDP growth and the Fed's inflation target (with potential GDP being the maximum level of output with a stable inflation rate). Global economic forces—such as the monetary policies of foreign central banks—can affect the neutral rate as well.

The current president of the Federal Reserve Bank of San Francisco, John Williams, is a leading thinker on the topic, and his work shows that the neutral rate has been declining for quite some time with about 50% of the decline attributable to lower potential growth. In other words, since the United States will grow more slowly, the neutral rate of interest must also be lower.

Interest rates do not live in a vacuum, and the US does not have the potential growth it once did. The Congressional Budget Office (CBO) estimates potential real GDP growth to be around 2% between 2015 and 2025. Interestingly, the FOMC's own projection for real GDP growth in the long run is about 2%. Both the Fed and the CBO have seen their estimates fall over time.

Part of the recent slowdown in potential GDP is due to lower productivity. And since the global economy just enjoyed a surge in productivity from the IT revolution, it should not be surprising that productivity has slowed. A slowing in the growth of the labor force would push potential GDP growth even lower than the current estimates—the CBO currently projects potential productivity growth at 1.6% and labor force growth at a half percent. This would be reduced by several factors, including lower labor-force participation. It is not hard to imagine one or both of these numbers being revised down to show slower potential growth.

Inflation is the other critical component of the policy neutral rate. It has not been a concern to Fed officials. There is little evidence of significant upward pressure on prices. And now there are questions being raised as to whether the Fed's 2% inflation target is high enough. The Fed talked about the neutral (equilibrium) interest rate at its April 2015 policy meeting.

> [S]ome participants reported that their estimates were currently unusually low by historical standards, reflecting, for example, factors weighing persistently on aggregate demand... One participant suggested that, in part because of the evidence that the equilibrium real interest rate was low by historical standards, **the Committee should discuss the possibility of increasing its longer-run inflation objective**. (emphasis added)

Remember, the neutral rate is a longer-term indicator and one that changes slowly. With the Fed attempting to guide markets off a bottom in rates, this may become their new "this time is different" tool for guiding markets about the future path of rates.

Assuming the neutral rate has fallen over the past several years, the eventual top of the coming rate-hike cycle should be lower. But the steepness of the path of hikes also matters, and expectations are important. The FOMC projects inflation will be below the 2% mark for some time, and long-run GDP estimates continue to trend downward. (Not to mention that falling potential growth makes current monetary policy "tighter" than it would otherwise be.)

In discussing where neutral is, where the hike cycle should end, and how long it will take to get there, the Fed seems to be developing a couple of new tools for controlling expectations about the future of *this* rate-hike cycle. Neutral has been falling for decades. There is a distinct lack of inflationary pressure. We are unlikely to see any material increase in potential GDP.

With less potential and a slower path, the guidance around the path of rates, and the requisite chatter about the data dependence could become one of the Fed's most important tools this cycle and next. Since the neutral interest rate has moved lower, bouncing off zero will be a normal, possibly frequent, occurrence. And in this case, the Fed being stuck in neutral may not be so bad after all.

Remember Those Different Sate Economies? The Fed's Policy Problem

The US economy as a whole as a single neutral rate, but different regions of the US likely have their own. This is one of the many conundrums the Fed faces when setting policy. The differing regions of the United States benefitted unequally from QE. These regions will not react identically to less accommodative or restrictive monetary policy. Further, QE and other extraordinary measures distorted the usual correlations between monetary policy and regional economies. By widening the disparity in economic conditions between regions, the aggregate statistics masked weakness in some areas with strength in others. This disparity poses a problem for the Fed as it attempts to prudently conduct monetary policy for whole of the US. The Fed designs one monetary policy to rule all, but the best monetary policy for the aggregate may be detrimental to some of the parts.

A recession may prove elusive for quite some time even as the Fed tightens its policy. But it is naïve to dismiss the notion of regional recessions or slowdowns that do not drag the nation as a whole into recession. This possibility is accentuated by the fragility of many regional economies in the wake of the great recession and tepid nature of some regional recoveries.

Regional deviations are nothing new. Neither are regional recessions. Though certainly not the first time it occurred, oil prices between 1985 and 1986 caused a significant recession in certain areas of the country with energy exposure, but the rest of the country fared fine—even prospering.

A study by the Fed found that monetary policy, specifically QE, had the greatest impact on regions that need it the least. With its focus on re-energizing the mortgage markets, regions with strong housing markets benefitted the most through the refinancing channel. Elsewhere, steep housing price declines precluded many homeowners from refinancing due to credit considerations. In other words, QE made those who suffered least better off.

There will always be regions of the United States where the desired or optimal monetary policy differs dramatically from the monetary policy chosen by the Fed. This should be expected in a country as broad and economically diverse as the US. A change in policy could have disparate effects across regions. It is unlikely economies in states like Texas and Oklahoma will react similarly to those in New York and New Jersey—especially given the difference in their experiences during the recovery.

For a monetary union to work well, the business cycles of the members should generally align. While the EU is an easy target of ridicule in this respect, the US is not much better. A study by the Federal Reserve Bank of St. Louis found that some states, including Texas, tend to be out of sync with the rest of the US' business cycle. Much of this deviation is due to oil exposure causing Texas and other oil driven regions to react differently to monetary policy actions than others.

Not only are Texas and its brethren out of step with the rest of the United States, a study from the Philadelphia Fed shows the "energy belt" (including Texas, Colorado, Oklahoma, and others) is least affected by unanticipated increases in interest rates. Energy driven economies benefit from a better economy, since demand for oil increases. Since rising interest rates tend to happen during economic upswings, the region should be less susceptible to monetary policy shocks. It is too early to determine the impact of the shale boom and bust and how it altered the oil belt's reaction to monetary policy.

The manufacturing sector is one of the more sensitive to interest rates. And this explains why the region commonly found to be the most sensitive to an interest rate hike is the Great Lakes region—closely overlapping the Rust Belt. With a durable goods manufacturing base, interest rate movements should have a considerable impact on economic activity. These types of purchases are heavily influenced by financing costs. If interest rates rise, these will be the industries quickly and deeply affected.

Regions with relatively healthy economies benefited disproportionately from non-conventional action. Economists agree that targeting regional effects with monetary policy is difficult, if not impossible. However, regional issues affecting monetary policy are not only a reasonable expectation but a norm that must be recognized and thoroughly understood when making policy choices. Monetary policy is forced to examine and react to aggregate level data, but it has real and tangible local effects.

An interesting question the Fed should consider in conducting policy would be whether the regions driving the recovery can withstand a hike, not whether the "United States" is strong enough for a rate hike. A less accommodative Fed may be putting the brakes on the regions that benefitted the least from its monetary actions, and not those that prospered. Either way, it needs to be recognized that these responses can have dramatic unintended consequences—positive or negative—on regional economic performance.

Global Doom and Local Boom

And the regionality of the US economy should be kept in mind when the concept of "secular stagnation" is broached. Secular stagnation is ill-defined. (It has a definition, but no one has stuck to it.) And by being somewhat ambiguous, it can mean different things to different people—which can be useful in crafting an argument. Broadly, secular stagnation is the theory that economic overhangs will slow global growth, resulting in slower growth for an extended period of time.

But like many professions, macroeconomists tend to fall into the fallacy of extrapolating broad trends into sweeping statements. These "stylized" versions of an economy are useful in some cases. In the case of secular stagnation, the characterizations are misleading. The subtleties are worth noting.

One of the more important side effects of stagnation is lower (neutral) interest rates as discussed earlier in the book. This leads to increased leverage and likely frequent run-ins with the "zero or lower" bound of interest rates and quantitative (or creative) easing, which are generally expansionary policies. That the global economy is muddling through does not imply that every economy everywhere will struggle.

When an economy is healthy, there are plenty of investment options. But when there are few opportunities and areas of growth, there tends to be some chasing of those returns. One example is the US shale boom. High oil prices were the result of QE, a weak dollar, and a technological step change in drilling for oil. Spurred by these, cheap debt and booming commodity prices led to what in retrospect was over-investment in the sector. With suppressed interest rates, the investment yields offered in the oil sector were attractive to investors. The money chased increasingly risky projects, and now—for a variety of reasons— oil is half the price it was at its peak a few years ago. Even in a time of secular stagnation, there are pockets of economic success.

Global doom and local boom can coexist. In some ways, secular stagnation may make the magnitude of local booms worse. "Local" is not simply geographic and it might be better termed as "niche." It may be a sector, such as virtual reality technology, or a region, such as Silicon Valley.

One could argue that the housing bubble was a classic example of this type of economic scenario. The US economy had few areas of true economic growth, but persistently low interest rates allowed for a significant bubble. Economists were stuck looking at the aggregate economic data. Few took the time to understand the underlying dynamics. Similar to the consequences of stagnation, excess leverage played a role. The pocket of boom turned to a dramatic bust.

Oddly, monetary policy was purported to have figured out how to mitigate or even avoid the harshest aspects of the business cycle. Now the business cycle may, in some ways, be harsher than it was previously. This is partly due to the Fed's zero-interest rate policy encouraging local booms. And until the Fed adjusts to this reality, localized bubbles may inflate and deflate more frequently. The Fed will have little ability to intervene.

The question then becomes how to react to this type of economic arrangement of little overall growth but pockets of boom. Without many economic growth points, there is a distinct likelihood of a boom causing problematic busts. And because of these dynamics, monetary policy becomes more complicated to undertake. Income and wage differentials are likely to spike across geographies. Employment levels and gains will be far less uniform than in previous economic cycles.

Furthermore, there are tremendous headwinds to the global economy as China slows and Europe ages. The global economy is not going to sustainably experience the high growth rates of the late 20th and early 21st century in the near future. Some of the headwinds are temporary. Others, though, such as demographics, are long-tailed and will take time to work through.

Even secular stagnation cannot stifle all good things all the time. Because there are so few investments and there is leverage to chase them, the low interest rates associated with secular stagnation make the booms more intense. And the Fed has little ability to control or deflate them, given the general weakness of the overall economy. Even if there is global doom, there will always be a local boom—somewhere.

Failure to Force a Thriving Economy

Partially due to long-term forces restraining growth, the US economy has grown painfully slowly over the past few years. The Federal Reserve has been blamed both for causing the financial crisis and for being too interventionist to correct its mistakes. Some in Congress aim to curtail the use of creative monetary policy by requiring the Fed to adhere to a formula that will set the Fed's key policy rate based on certain economic data points—a "policy rule."

Legitimate reasons and concerns underlie the push toward an explicit rule for monetary policy. Extraordinary intervention during the financial crisis caused many to question the boundaries of the Fed's emergency powers. More positively, it seems reasonable to assume that monetary policy might function and transmit to the economy more efficiently if the Fed is required to follow a predictable rule.

There have been a few proposed pieces of legislation. One was known as the Federal Reserve Accountability and Transparency Act (FRAT). In testimony before a congressional committee, John Taylor—arguably the godfather of the monetary policy rule—laid out his support for a systematic rule to guide Federal Reserve decision making.

This should surprise no one, since some proposed legislation even includes something called "The Taylor Rule" as a reference point for monetary policy. Taylor's namesake aims to keep the Fed honest and ensure monetary policy is reasonable and prudent.

Part of the argument rests on the notion that monetary policy works best when there are clear goals and the arbiters of policy are open about how—and why—they are making their decisions. The Taylor rule takes into account the neutral real rate, inflation, and the output gap. In theory, this sounds good, but in practice there are complications.

The Fed already provides targets for inflation and unemployment—the two sides of their dual mandate. And the targets have and will continue to change. As discussed earlier, some members of the FOMC have suggested an increase in the target inflation rate above the standard 2%. The unemployment rate target has already declined as the economy improved. The economy evolves and the targets should too. Sometimes these targets may need to move in politically unfavorable directions. This could become a political firestorm.

The US dollar is central to global trade. US monetary policy does not act in a vacuum. Other central banks pay close attention to the dollar's value relative to their local currencies. The Taylor Rule and other mechanical monetary-policy tools are useful for conducting a sort of *ceteris paribus* (all things being equal) closed-economy monetary policy—the type of policy that neither exists nor is relevant in practice. But when combined with explicit targets and increased transparency, close adherence to a policy rule encourages cheating by others who are not so constrained. This complicates the ability of the Fed to accomplish prudent policy without undue political influence.

Beyond the problems associated with following a FRAT-like measure, implementation and political understanding of a policy rule will be difficult. For instance, the Fed will inevitably overshoot and undershoot inflation and unemployment. How much variance is acceptable? Will there be consequences for missing these targets? According to the FRAT, the Fed will be allowed to designate a "directive" rule to articulate to the public. If the Fed's rule deviates from the prescriptions of the Taylor Rule or whatever rule it chooses, the Fed will have to explain and justify the differential. What if the Taylor Rule would have failed to achieve the desired policy outcome? Would the reference rate be reviewed?

Creating a rules-based system with checks against deviation may actually cause more harm to the Fed's credibility by showing consistent gaps between targets and reality. Sharp, unanticipated shifts from longer-term goals could cause severe harm to the economy. The legislation purports to bring more transparency and stability. But without significant flexibility built around the targets, the opposite outcome could occur, as policy targets would be frequently revisited and revised.

The Taylor Rule is not a cure all. At the beginning of 2016, the calculation from the Taylor Rule indicated that the fed funds rate should be approximately 2%. Considering fed funds were near 0% at that point, there was a wide deviation. There are several ways to interpret and modify the formula. Former Fed Chair Ben Bernanke used core PCE (personal consumption expenditures) inflation in his calculation and changed the weighting given to the output gap, completely altering the outcome.

The output gap requires that potential GDP be estimated. This can lead to significant deviations from period to period. When the San Francisco Fed published its survey of seven different output gaps, they ranged from –2.6% using CBO calculations to +2.4% using job vacancies. Plugging in one instead of the other would change the suggested interest rate policy drastically. And we cannot forget the large and potentially policy-changing revisions to the relevant data series over long periods of time. Even if there were an agreed-upon calculation of the output gap for the reference rate, the revisions to the data would likely render the first look useless for setting policy.

The Fed wields a tremendous amount of economic power in its monetary policy. If Congress wants to talk to the chair of the Fed more often, that should be encouraged. But monetary policy rules are confusing, unreliable, and easily manipulated using different data. Data nuances and oddities could go from being an interesting study to causing a recession or putting undue and unnecessary political pressure on the Fed. Asking for more transparency is fine, but asking the Fed to conduct itself using a policy rule is counterproductive.

More Participation Trophies

And a policy rule may find that some of the current data distortions lead to particularly poor policy outcomes. Even so, maybe it is time to consider giving out participation trophies. It worked on Millennials. Why not the rest of the economy? Since 2000, participation in the labor force has been declining and will continue to do so. In the current political environment, with the Trump administration stressing the creation of jobs and a return of manufacturing to the United States, this trend is likely to become a lightning rod. But it shouldn't be.

The president and his nominees have already opined on the validity of other labor statistics, with the Treasury secretary calling the unemployment rate "not real" and Trump suggesting when he was a presidential candidate that the unemployment rate "is probably 28, 29, as high as 35."

Certainly, the methodology behind arriving at the headline unemployment number can be debated. There could be an argument for a figure around 10%—adding people who work part time and want a full-time job, together with those who have become discouraged and are "marginally attached." That figure, published by the US Bureau of Labor Statistics as the U-6 measure, currently sits at more than 8%. But there is no justification for a number north of 20%.

What do comments relating to the unemployment rate have to do with a declining participation rate? Quite a bit. A decline in labor force participation places downward pressure on the unemployment rate. With a labor force in transition, a jobs-first president would need a reversal or at least a stabilization of the trend to continue to create jobs at the current fairly rapid pace.

But reversing the trend with any sustainability would require changing the demographics of the United States. The Atlanta Federal Reserve looked at people who decided not to participate. Since the fourth quarter of 2007, the participation rate has fallen by more than 3%, with most of the decline tied to structural and noncyclical demographic factors. Very little is associated with being discouraged and choosing to leave. This "shadow labor force" contributed less than 0.5% of the decline.

To give an idea of where the fall in participation has come from since the Great Recession began, the Atlanta Fed looked at the range of underlying drivers. Aging of the population is the primary contributor. This should not be a surprise. Boomers are aging out of their working years and into retirement. When you retire, you fall out of the labor force but not out of the over-16 noninstitutionalized population. This drives down labor force participation by reducing the numerator but not the denominator.

For context, since the fourth quarter of 2007, population aging is responsible for nearly two-thirds of the fall in participation—2.1 percentage points of the 3.2%. Other contributors to the lower rate are health issues and people delaying work to go to school. Those two combine for 1.5%. The evolution of the labor force demands more time spent in school. And the aging of the population is not a shock to observers who have been watching the boomer generation for years.

So, aging is irreversible, schooling is a necessity, and little can be done to reverse the downward participation trend. But it is not all dire. There have actually been factors that bolstered participation in the labor force since the Great Recession.

The most intriguing trend is the postponement of retirement by some of the boomers. Whether it is a result of a shock to their savings from asset prices or the loss of anticipated income, some boomers are putting off their retirement. This has the effect of holding back part of the flood of age-related participation declines. Cumulatively, this equates to increasing participation by nearly 1%. One question is when will people be less likely to delay retirement. The additional pressure from more retirements could weigh on participation quickly.

Following the Great Recession, participation among those with family responsibilities increased. This encompasses individuals who had previously stayed home to raise children or care for family members. In absolute terms, the labor force is not shrinking. But as a portion of the employable population, it is shrinking and will continue to do so. This has little if anything to do with a shortage of jobs and lots to do with the aging of America. According to the Job Openings and Labor Turnover Survey, there are more than five million job openings.

The reality is that the US economy and its employment structure have shifted. The population is getting older, and more education delays entry into the labor force. Because the labor force is growing more slowly and its requirements are evolving, creating a jobs boom in America will prove difficult—even with participation trophies.

After Normal, Fed Edition

Now for the Greenspan Trap

In the late 20th century and the first decade of the 21st, Alan Greenspan led a Fed that—in retrospect—kept monetary policy loose for a very long period of time. Inflation was tame. Wage pressures were nonexistent due to the acceleration of global competition for jobs and the relocation of American manufacturing jobs to China. Seeing none of the typical indicators of an overheated economy, low interest rates seemed a reasonable means to spur job creation and spark some wage inflation.

The result was a housing bubble. And housing created the type of low or non-contestable jobs that were impossible to find in other sectors of the economy—construction. Housing construction jobs were easy transitions from the manufacturing floor. And they could not be taken offshore easily. They were China proof. But the housing bubble burst in spectacular fashion. The inflation—except in home prices—never materialized. And Greenspan is given credit (blame) for building the housing bubble.

Today, the mystery of low inflation is creating complications for the Fed again. China's surprise move to devalue the yuan had a profound effect on the global economy in 2015. Deflationary pressures were exported to countries who import Chinese goods, which in turn affected monetary policy decisions in those countries. The US economy and the Fed were not immune to these forces. Deflationary pressures gave the Fed pause as it moved toward lifting interest rates off zero. It was not the ECB or BoJ that broke the Yellen Accord. It was China. It all felt a bit too familiar. Without care, the Fed could have fallen into the Greenspan Trap—again.

There are reasons to be skeptical of the People's Bank of China (PBoC)'s timing. The "one-off" reset of the yuan was certainly an unexpected move. But the critical aspect of the move was the shift in the mechanism for setting the "fix" (the target value of the yuan against the dollar). Instead of being set unilaterally by the PBoC and allowed to move very little, the yuan was allowed to be, in part, set by market forces—a move the IMF had been calling for ahead of China's inclusion in its Special Drawing Rights. The resetting of the yuan's value had only just begun.

The yuan drifted lower over an extended period (for most of 2016), advanced economies felt the deflationary pressure through commodity and import channels. China will became incrementally more competitive with other emerging nations. For the United States, it means deflationary pressures from the Middle Kingdom will last for some time. This is not dissimilar from the long, slow offshoring of manufacturing that kept wages and inflation in check in the Greenspan Era.

For the Fed, this created a bit of a dilemma. The US economy had steadily created jobs, but inflation and wage growth disappointed. Greenspan's low rates were a result of the terrorist attacks of 9/11. His Fed faced a trickle of jobs and a competitive threat to the vestige of American manufacturing.

This time around the Fed had already kept rates low for a long time, drawing criticism and even threats of congressional oversight. China, instead of taking jobs, was moving toward a market mechanism to determine exchange rates. (It probably wanted to get ahead of the Fed rate hike.)

The potential deflationary forces from the Chinese devaluation probably tempted the Fed to delay lifting off. However, the Fed did not fall into the Greenspan trap this time around. Regardless of what the Fed chooses to do, there will be deflationary pressures as China's growth slows.

Even before the yuan began its revaluation, the Fed was up against significant policy headwinds from other large trading partners. Europe and Japan were both undergoing large-scale easing. China was merely playing catch-up with recent currency moves. It was only natural for China to join the fray. Regardless of the high visibility of the devaluation of the yuan, it should be thought of in a much broader context of the strong US dollar.

The current Fed heeded the lesson of history. The risks appeared benign and nonexistent until they were malignant and obvious. Low inflation could have been used as an excuse to push out a lift-off. China has exported disinflation to trading partners before and it will do so again. The mechanism was different this time, but the deflationary pressures the same. Yes, the Greenspan Trap is tempting but should be resisted. The difficulty lies in explaining this to the Fed watchers, markets, and the general public. Otherwise, history repeats and the US will eventually find another subprime mess or shale boom somewhere it does not want it.

Clouding the Mandate and Forward Guidance

How did the Fed deal with the Greenspan Trap? All eyes were on a September 2015 rate hike. But a close examination of the minutes from the meeting leading up to it suggested that the FOMC had not made up its mind. The Fed's ambivalence was not surprising, but some of the nondomestic reasons for it—China, oil, and the strong dollar—were.

Of course the minutes also cited stubbornly low domestic inflation and a general lack of upward wage pressures as concerns for raising rates too early. The problem? The Greenspan Trap and a strong dollar complicated the Fed's ability to properly operate, given it is tasked with achieving economic targets only in the United States—not globally.

When topics concerning the global economy were raised, they were carefully grounded in their particular interaction with the US economy. Take one comment on how FOMC participants were thinking about the evolution of the dollar as they began to hike rates.

> "Some participants also discussed the risk that a possible divergence in interest rates in the United States and abroad might lead to further appreciation of the dollar, extending the downward pressure on commodity prices and the weakness in net exports."

No mention is made of the capital flight from the emerging world in the face of a rising dollar or the slowdown in commodity producing countries due to lower prices for their exports. The concentration, rightly so given the US-centric mandate, is only on the US.

This begs the question: "Was the Fed simply making an attempt to placate other central banks that fear Fed actions could destroy their domestic economies? Or was the Fed being far coyer and attempting to become independent of its mandated targets by creating a new, more pressing but vague one?"

The answer is probably a bit of both. Given its dual mandate targets, the Fed could and possibly should include international feedback in its policy decision matrix. But for a variety of reasons, the Fed may want to use the global macro concerns as a viable, nebulous reason to alter policy direction when it becomes strategically useful to do so. It may also allow the Fed to only slowly raise rates until some semblance of wage pressures and inflation reemerge. But there is also a bit of a friendly warning embedded in the global mandate. In diverging from the global easing policies of other central banks, the Fed is aware of what damage it can cause to the emerging world. But the Fed will act anyway. Countries should prepare for it.

In choosing to debate the effects of Fed policy on the global economy, however, the Fed invited speculation into whether its guideposts for policy tightening has moved, putting itself (farther) into an impossible spot. If the Fed continued to use more of a "prudential global macro" policy to guide markets, it would become increasingly difficult to maintain credibility in future policy decisions. (There is usually a reason to ease or do nothing. Risks are abundant, and there are frequently reasons to tighten policy. Bubbles are everywhere!) Consistently stressing the global element of monetary policy would also raise the question of whether the Fed should be concerned about anything outside of its dual mandate. (Oil prices and net exports have a direct effect on their dual mandate through inflation and employment.)

One of the primary risks of muddling the mandate: If all the guideposts are met domestically and the Fed does not raise interest rates, it risks signaling a weak domestic economic background. This is something of a self-fulfilling prophecy. However, there are short-term benefits to not raising rates. Downward pressure on the dollar and upward pressure on commodity prices could boost the US economy. When the US economy began to falter in early 2016, the tactic of lowering interest rate hike expectations through forward guidance of global risks was successfully deployed. The US dollar, which has strengthened drastically over the past couple years, moved lower. Oil prices recovered. And US growth bounced.

But this scenario was not ideal for much of the world. Central banks in Japan and Europe were easing policy significantly. The quick pivot by the Fed away from tightening lowered the efficacy of their monetary policies. By paying attention to global stability and the effects of a stronger dollar, the Fed likely caused other central banks to further increase their stimulus policies. In turn, this made it even more difficult for the Fed to normalize its policy regime creating an accidental feedback loop.

The Fed wanted to appear prudent in its monetary policies—and avoid blame for another bubble. So much so, the guideposts for its initial rate hike—previously a mixture of employment and inflation indicators—included global macro variables that are outside the direct purview of monetary policy. Being concerned with the global economy makes the Fed's task, which is already difficult, impossible. And in the case of lifting off of its zero interest rate policy, a global perspective unnecessarily muddied the waters and complicated the process.

Default Settings

Monetary policy is not the only culprit in causing policies to be suboptimal. Congress has gotten into the habit of using the debt ceiling as a political weapon. A point will be reached when it will not matter that "the US is not going to default this time." Eventually, playing with the debt ceiling increases the risk that it could happen by accident. And an accidental default would have disastrous results on the US' credibility and legitimacy. Though not immediately viable, the recently added reserve currency—the Chinese yuan or RMB—could become more favored due to political instability in the US. This is not necessarily a bad thing, but it does have consequences.

Were the US to accidentally default on a portion of its debt (and in most scenarios it would likely be only a portion), interest rates on US Treasuries could increase substantially, threatening the US' ability to refinance its debt at reasonable interest rates later. This would place the remaining US debt on watch and, without the ability to roll debt over, put the US in a precarious position. There is some likelihood that this scenario could alter the aforementioned favorable interest payments-to-revenue equation and cause instability in global financial markets.

A loss of confidence from the global investors who fund the US deficit would have profound consequences. So profound that the Fed has a plan in place to mitigate the fallout from an accidental default. The solution? Basically ignoring that there is a problem and continuing to accept Treasuries as collateral for borrowing. And the Fed can do this because a default would *have* to be temporary—a game of political chicken gone wrong or an unintentional hiccup in the payments system. A true default is simply inconceivable.

The US political system is increasingly fractious. Each round of debt ceiling chicken increases the possibly of "perceived true default." The consequences of a perceived true default—not simply a technical, short-term one—in which investors and the Fed have little to no view into how the situation will resolve itself, is where the true, permanent damage to the US economy occurs.

Defaulting on the debt does not simply risk a spike in US interest rates and cause future debt payments to become rapidly unsustainable. A glitch in the sanctity of US debt would accelerate the shift toward a more bipolar economic and monetary order, with the US and the dollar on one side and China and the RMB on the other.

Inclusion in the IMF's SDR is part and parcel to the attempt to internationalize the yuan. Some trading partners may enjoy the prospect of having less exposure to the US dollar in the future. But if the US defaults, the diversification away from the dollar would be far more pronounced. In the case of a dollar default, it would be difficult for much of the world—especially the emerging world—to justify their over-reliance and allocation to the dollar. The PBoC is already beginning to allow the yuan to float more in line with what the free market would dictate—regardless of how bungled and poorly communicated the initial stages of the transition were.

Meanwhile, the Fed is already a villain to some parts of the emerging world. There, the Fed's QE and interest rate policies built bubbles, and in some cases, the reversal of its stance popped them. Many central banks would prefer to have a viable second reserve currency to keep the other in check. If there were two, one bad actor could more easily be punished. Theoretically, with the yuan a viable contender, central bank reserve holdings would begin to diversify into non-US dollar assets and currencies. And this reduces the demand for US debt in the long run.

A default on the US debt would cause problems in the domestic economy as financial and asset markets melted down. Further, US government borrowing costs could potentially make the US deficit and debt unsustainable much sooner than otherwise. But the most outcome prominent outcome would be the acceleration of the rise of a more bipolar monetary order. At the moment, the global reserve currency is the US dollar. (Though not the only, it remains dominant.) And the US enjoys great benefits from it. Perpetually playing chicken with the debt ceiling and creditor credibility could risk sparking a "flight to others" as the safety of US Treasury bills and by extension the dollar becomes a thing of the past.

The Global Middle Class at Risk

From the perspective of the emerging world, however, the threat of a temporary default on the US debt is not the most troubling development of the after normal world. In recent years, the emerging world—lower and middle income countries alike—found China's insatiable appetite for commodities a godsend. For the new middle class, the resultant commodity super-cycle was the simplest route to plenty. If a country had commodities, it benefited—either from direct trade or though persistently higher prices of nearly all industrial commodities. By meeting China's surging demand, the global middle class was going to grow forever.

According to Pew Research Center data, this global middle class—a bracket including those making between $10.01 and $20 per day on an adjusted basis—grew from 7% of the global population in 2001 to 13% in 2011. That's not something to be disappointed about. The low-income bracket—$2.01 to $10 per day—increased from 50% to 56%. The rapid decline in the percentage of the world's poor, from 29% to 15%, is quite the feat. But it is not the entire story.

As pointed out by Pew, more than half of the new global middle class was created in China. Using the same dataset as Pew, that means 203 million of the 386 million who joined the middle class were in China. The figure is astounding but not surprising. The scale of Chinese economic growth was not only lifting its own citizens out of poverty but also—through its increasing demand—the rest of the world. In many ways, there is no "global" middle class. There is a "Chinese" middle class that spills over China's borders.

But commodity growth is easy growth. And China is in the midst of a pivot away from the construction and manufacturing underpinnings of its immense growth. This has caused commodities to crash. The prevailing thesis of a new emerging middle class—and the accompanying expectations of higher demand for developed world goods and services—must be reexamined and possibly, revised.

Brazil, Chile, Venezuela, Peru, and Argentina have significant export ties with China. This consists mostly of soybeans, iron ore, copper, and oil. Brazil alone added nearly 24 million people to its middle class as trade with China grew many times over in recent years. The economic reliance of much of South America on commodities further exacerbates its dependence on Chinese growth. But the equation is rather simple: As China slows its infrastructure investment, commodity prices fall under pressure.

Mexico, an outlier among the countries that made progress, lifted 12.9 million into its middle class while exporting little to China. Mexico does, however, have a significant petroleum industry. But the upheaval caused by the emergence and spread of hydraulic fracturing in the United States and the resultant lower oil prices may make it more difficult to grow a middle class. Still, thus far, Mexico has fared relatively well considering the slow growth in the US and low oil prices.

Economists have long observed the difficulty of moving from "middle income" to "upper income." This is a problem known as the "middle income trap." Somewhat more disturbing, there now appears to be a lower likelihood of moving up the ranks in low-income countries as well. Simply, a country that starts as a low-income country is likely to stay there. (The same holds true for the high-income brackets.) A recent St. Louis Fed study by Maria Arias and Yi Wen found a 5% chance of transitioning from low to middle and an 18% chance of middle to high—over 140 years.

Even with all its growth, China is still a low-income country. India, which has made tremendous strides in alleviating poverty, increased its low-income bracket far more than its middle income cohort. Meanwhile, Africa, both on the whole and reduced into its individual parts, is disappointing. Nigeria, with its rich commodity endowment, has lagged, with little transition to the middle class. Outside of China's sphere of influence, the global middle class has gained little. Even under extraordinarily positive conditions, the upward shift is difficult to execute.

It may be too simplistic to blame the demise of the global middle class on China's abrupt pivot and a declining commodity market. In many ways, emerging countries themselves deserve to bear some of the blame. The fleetingness of the commodity boom was recognized by few and exploited without much heed for the future. Only time will tell if those countries who reached the middle class during the boom years can stay there and whether or not China's focus on growing its domestic consumer economy can sustain its own middle class.

The emerging world faces not only a commodity bust and a slowdown in China but now the potential for increasingly tight—though still historically loose—monetary policy in the United States. Higher US interest rates encourage capital flows to exit the emerging world, exacerbating the existing problem.

The rise of the global middle class has been taken as a given. But its rise is slowing and may even be over. The surge in incomes and consumption by the developing world may be more anomaly than trajectory. Commodities are cyclical after all. The global middle class may prove to be as well. At least until the next China comes along.

And Then China Slowed

Waiting for the next China may be a long wait. And global growth is certainly unlikely to be jolted by the US, barring surprisingly aggressive tax reform. Larry Summers has suggested that the US economy is mired in a permanently lower trajectory of growth called "secular stagnation." Well, maybe. This assertion is certainly not without its own merit. There have been loud expressions of both agreement and disagreement. Using his newly acquired ability to blog, former Federal Reserve Chair Ben Bernanke came out staunchly against the notion. But the US economy itself has produced little evidence to counter Summers' theory as of late. The debate rages on.

To Bernanke, Summers' argument fails by ignoring the international aspects of US economic growth. But the recent deterioration in China and emerging world economies reduces the overall forcefulness of this objection. Bernanke was correct to critique Summers' lack of international perspective, but secular stagnation is more than a US phenomenon. In fact, the global economy as a whole may well have already slipped into a much slower growth mode.

China drove the global economy for 15 years. But—though the official data is erroneous and private estimates vary widely—China's growth has meaningfully slowed. Leaving the world to search for other drivers of growth. But there are no countries, no growth stories waiting in the wings to carry the global economy to new heights. Or far more frightening, to maintain the current growth trajectory. This should be of particular concern to those expecting—wishing for—any sort of acceleration. Few know the true health of the Chinese economy, but the pivot of the world's second largest economy will have a huge impact.

Secular stagnation may have been covered up by the Chinese growth juggernaut. Or possibly, the let-down from China's growth is giving the illusion of secular stagnation. Either way, the scope of the slowdown is enormous. Using figures from the IMF that adjust for purchasing power, the Chinese economy should contribute growth of at least $1 trillion to the global economy for the foreseeable future. This is a sizable portion of global growth.

The emerging world, a recent source of economic strength, will struggle to pick up the slack of a Chinese slowdown—partly due to a reliance on exports of commodities to China. The emerging world's quick snap back from the Great Recession has more to do with its commodity endowments and developed market monetary policy than anything else. Emerging markets have no institutions or the needed governance to properly cope with even a moderate deceleration of Chinese commodity consumption.

Commodities, primarily oil, have played a significant role in the US economic recovery as well, stimulating capital spending and employment. This will be remembered as a bubble driven by Fed policies that maintained low interest rates, a weak dollar, and high oil prices. The surge in employment due to oil field and related jobs—mostly high paying—masked an even weaker underlying recovery in the US.

By most estimates, US potential growth has declined below 2%. This is from a combination of slower population growth and productivity. It indicates that even the current lackluster US economic performance may be above its longer-term potential.

Meanwhile, the rest of the developed world fits neatly into Summers' notion of secular stagnation. Europe is sitting well below the zero lower bound with a significant, and possibly extending, QE program to spur growth and inflation. Neither growth nor inflation has made an appearance yet. Japan has been approaching monetary policy the same way for the better part of the 21st century. Both economies are disappointments, and their potential growth is probably far lower than economists would like to admit.

Economic growth should come more easily to India than to China (and the rest of the world for that matter), but India's democracy is incapable of mustering the scale of development China's totalitarian regime could. Its growth will be at a far more measured pace. It is unlikely to have the same type of surge that China did.

The possibility of a permanent or semi-permanent lower potential growth for the United States, Europe, and Japan is neither controversial nor surprising. But China's troubles seem to have come as a shock to much of the world. The architects of an incredible economic rise unparalleled in economic history, the Politburo and the PBoC now have some battle scars from their handling of the so far moderate liberalization of the yuan and the subsequent precipitous volatility in their domestic stock market.

And confidence in the ability of the Chinese government to pivot their economy from labor-intensive manufacturing to higher-value-added activities and consumption is eroding. China has built its capacity to produce steel and concrete. There is little confidence it has created the capacity for knowledge-based industries—yet. Suddenly, there is far less confidence that growth will materialize.

Wholesale economic collapse does not appear to be, and should not be, on the horizon. But the four major economic powers—the US, Japan, the EU, and China—appear to be sliding into their own unique forms of secular stagnation. With potential catalysts—such as the TTIP—looking ever less likely, the chances for the West to escape a prolonged period of slow growth (or worse) are fading.

China has many levers to pull economically, and stagnation and lower potential growth are relative. But the global hunt for economic growth by central banks will be a persistent source of volatility in financial markets. Without the ability to jump-start their economies using traditional monetary policy instruments, central banks will use unconventional policies more often in attempts to remain globally competitive and search for increasingly elusive growth spurts. Unfortunately for the global economy, Larry Summers was correct.

The Fed's Cred

"The Fed is tightening at the wrong time" is an argument that holds water in nearly all circumstances, and honestly, this is nearly guaranteed to be true. "Perfect timing" and "monetary policy" should never be used in the same sentence. There is always a reason to wait or move ahead or pause. The question that should be asked about Fed policy is not about optimal timing (timing never is), but whether it did or will do more good than harm. Arguing for a rate hike or policy tightening generally is far harder than wait-and-see or loosening.

If arguing the "good" side of policy tightening, one must make the awkward case that a rate hike helps avoid a hypothetical future "harm." (i.e., "If the Fed had not hiked, it would have been bad.") In a way, the Fed may already be acknowledging the difficulty through its emphasis on a gradual pace of normalization. This shows that its motivations are not the traditional slowing of the economy and reduction of inflationary pressures but the amorphous goal of "normalization." Inflation is certainly not an imminent threat to the US economy. Employment may be reaching "full," but the level of employment this constitutes is debatable, as is the term "normal." The Fed does not want to stifle the economic recovery, but if it truly wishes to normalize, it may have no choice.

If the Fed is not successful in normalizing rates, its monetary policy options (outside of new rounds of QE or derivatives thereof) are severely limited in the event that some external shock rocks the US economy into a recession. The risk of asset price overshoots—or "bubbles"—would continue to increase. The argument for why the Fed should be keen to marginally normalize policy to prepare for a shock seems esoteric, even self-defeating.

Demonizing the normalization process does not take the same esoteric type of argument. It is much simpler, and the risks are more concrete. Very simply, the Fed cannot afford to have the economy fall into a recession too soon after starting its "normalization." Foremost, it would risk its own credibility, an indication that the Fed misread the strength and sustainability of the US economy.

A legitimate fear is an increase in encounters with zero interest-rate policy (ZIRP). If the Fed acts too hastily and slows the economy or the US dollar strengthens too much, or a combination of the two, the Fed would find itself not only returning to ZIRP, but also some form of QE. It might likely target long-term rates similar to the post-World War II experience (and Japan today). It would then have to delay further moves until the economy had healed. The US economy would find itself in a sort of "Groundhog Day" scenario. Moving too fast will bring fallout that the Fed has probably considered but cannot easily prepare for.

In any event, it will take the Fed a long time to move rates much without damaging the US recovery. It took years to get slightly over 1% and begin talking about reducing the balance sheet. Another longer-term and more persistent headwind for the Fed is the decline in potential US GDP and the requisite falling neutral Fed policy rate. The result is less operating room for the Fed than in previous cycles. The Fed has to be more sensitive to potential economic shocks.

Torpedoing the economy would unwind the good faith that Volcker and others built for the Fed—its credibility thoroughly and utterly destroyed. In the 1980s Chairman Paul Volcker singlehandedly caused a recession, broke inflation, and gained the Fed an incredible amount of trust. It will be lost in a scenario where the Fed is quickly forced to return to QE. And worse, without credibility the Fed may not be able to spark the type of outcome it needs even with large amounts of stimulus. Without its credibility, many of the Fed's tools—from forward guidance to QE—would become far less useful. This is a potentially tragic outcome and repairing the damage an unfathomable task.

Moving toward normalization and neutral is a good idea in theory. But the Fed and the US economy are by no means out of the woods. Relapsing to ZIRP and QE are risks that warrant acknowledgement from the Fed. It is time to understand that normality—whatever it is—is still a long way off.

There Are No Big Guns Left

The Fed is in the middle of a debate of its own creation: How do policy makers approach a slow growing US economy? Given its mandate, the Fed has had little choice but to undertake QE and maintain its 0% or near 0% since December 2008. From the perspective of the Fed, the United States has weathered the storm well thus far, given the number of hurdles—a strengthening dollar and policy tightening since the mid-2014 taper, to name a couple. Now as the world focuses on the Fed's tightening to neutral stance, the Fed must consider the price it has paid for its interventions.

There are two principal reasons for this: demand exhaustion and excess (aggregate) supply.

Exhaustion and saturation are products of a limited capacity by governments and individuals to consume. Inspired by low interest rates, governments and consumers have leveraged themselves and are not in a position to dramatically reaccelerate their consumption patterns. In the US, debt service payments as a percentage of income are hovering near record-low levels. But consumer debt levels continue to increase. And significant amount of the borrowing is related to student loans, which cannot be reduced through the bankruptcy process. Low interest rates have helped to refinance and lower the ongoing burden of the obligations, but there has been minimal deleveraging. This is not merely a US phenomenon. Lower rates have pushed the cost of carrying debt down virtually everywhere.

For the Fed, demand exhaustion means a low or even zero interest rate policy will do little to spur further economic activity from consumers. Even within interest rate-sensitive sectors, there are disparate outcomes. Autos recovered well, but housing has lagged. Autos now appear to be a potential source of exhaustion. Demand exhaustion reduces the efficacy of the Fed's interest rate tool and forces a reconsideration of how to steer the US economy in coming cycles.

More worrying is the threat of excess aggregate supply. When interest rates are low, the hurdle is also low for investment returns, which encourages investment in marginal and speculative projects. This in turn leads to increases in supply—sometimes beyond what the market is able to absorb—leading to a glut. And a supply glut can have deflationary effects. Much of the argument for the Fed maintaining its zero interest rate policy has been to spark inflation. Still, a significant amount of capital chasing marginal projects can add future deflationary pressures to the economic system.

The US oil patch is an example of how the excess aggregate supply dynamic works. One consequence of easy monetary policy is a weaker currency. The Fed has been on an easy money path for the majority of this century. And though occasionally interrupted, the dollar generally declined in value against major currencies between 2002 and 2011. Because commodities are generally priced in dollars, the weaker dollar pushed oil prices higher. A revitalized US oil industry boomed as high commodity prices combined with cheap financing and new technologies dramatically altered the supply curve.

And this is why excessive time at ZIRP may have been a problem. The US shale boom was successful enough to alter the geopolitics of oil and create an entirely new regime. Oil was expensive enough to drill in marginal places. And debt was cheap enough to take the risks. The result was a completely altered supply picture for oil. Suddenly, there was too much oil. To compensate, oil prices have fallen dramatically—a deflationary force.

The US economy has survived the financial crisis. In a world with few catalysts to compensate for a slowing China and the emerging world, the US economy's slow growth is enviable. But by pushing on ZIRP for too long, the Fed may have pulled forward all of the consumption it could and at the same time spurred too much capacity in the few areas where returns of magnitude were achievable. In other words, the price paid may have been the Fed's ability to successfully intervene in the future. It can always intervene, but the question will be how successfully.

But There Are Always Bullets Somewhere

The idea seems laughable now, but when the 21st century began, the Congressional Budget Office (CBO) was projecting that the United States would pay off its debt owed to the public by the middle of the present decade. Per the CBO's January 1999 *Economic and Budget Outlook*, "The long-term projections indicate that debt held by the public, driven by continued budget surpluses, will fall below zero by 2012." Today, debt held by the public is more than $14 trillion, so we didn't quite make it. But though the idea of less (or no) debt seems unambiguously positive from a fiscal perspective, it raises serious, fundamental questions from the viewpoint of monetary policy.

The one of the Fed's classic, go-to monetary policy instruments is the buying and selling of government debt to increase or decrease the risk-free rate. And at the start of the new millennium, the Fed was facing a future without it. Concerned about the potential fallout, it commissioned a study to look at possible alternatives. It is unfortunate in some ways that the United States did not sustain the path of its debt pay-down. But the alternatives that the Fed came up with back then may provide some insight into how QE policy may evolve in the future, when central banks' ability to purchase government debt has been effectively exhausted.

Back then, the Fed's explorations led to greater use of repurchase agreements. This is a tool the Fed uses extensively to control reserves as it works to get further away from the zero lower bound. Also, the now-infamous agency market (Fannie Mae, Freddie Mac, and similar entities) was beginning to emerge as an ever larger and more important market in mid-1999. For economists searching for the asset class to replace US Treasuries, these agencies and government-sponsored entities were the logical choice.

In some ways, the issues facing the Federal Reserve and other central banks today—and possibly tomorrow—are not entirely dissimilar to those at the turn of the century. Obviously, the United States did not pay down its debt. But the issue of how to conduct monetary policy when the primary markets and instruments it uses to do so are no longer relevant strikes at the heart of the Fed's struggle to enact and enforce its policy decisions as the US economy continues to evolve.

After all, the Fed can purchase only so many Treasuries before the market begins to look illiquid and unsuitable for transmitting policy back to the real economy—like it did in 1999 and 2000.

Some have leveled the claim that the Fed is "out of bullets" and no longer has the ability to ease policy to any meaningful extent. But statements like this ignore that the Fed has not only done the research on how to operate in a world after Treasuries, but that it has already purchased mortgage-backed securities and can simply request the ability to purchase other assets. In the after normal economy, the Fed may have to look to these ideas during future crises.

One potential is that vast majority of future QE purchases will be targeted at those assets the Fed labeled as able to be "benchmarks." This includes securities with deep and liquid markets that affect the prices of other assets, such as agencies and even some corporate names. This makes the assets similar in many ways to US Treasuries, making them attractive for the Fed to purchase. The Fed cannot buy corporate bonds. It would have to ask permission to do so from Congress. But it can buy almost everything else: bonds from agencies and some state and local governments, foreign currency, and foreign sovereign debt. This is a tremendously large pool of securities—the Fed will not run out of things to purchase.

So, the Fed has already looked into how it would conduct monetary policy when Treasuries dried up. When it needs to ease policy again, there will be plenty of room left to buy more Treasuries while leaving some for other market participants. There is no reason to fear, in the age of abundant debt, that the Fed is by any means out of bullets and out of options.

Easing the Night Away

Regardless of having near endless bullets, the truism remains: Monetary policy cannot solve every economic problem. After the glut of global QE, the assertion has probably never been more accurate. Eventually, reality could pose a problem for the Fed, the ECB, and others as they combat future recessions or crises of confidence. But there is also the potential for monetary policy to become—continue to be—far more relevant in determining global economic winners and losers than it has been in recent history. And monetary policy determining winners and losers is a deeply disturbing prospect.

With few methods left to spur growth, economies are heavily reliant on central bank actions to maintain even modest growth. ECB President Mario Draghi has made it clear the ECB is prepared to increase its level of stimulus to reflate the euro economy. A statement maintained even while rumors concerning the possible winding down of the ECB's stimulus program swirled. And the Bank of Japan, which exemplifies the perils of over reliance on monetary policy, is likely to experiment with creative monetary policy as long as the market will allow it. Japan is likely to push the bounds farther as inflation persists below its target. Even the Fed, cited global economic events as an excuse for delaying a widely anticipated rate hike at its September 2015 meeting and rediscovered it during the tumult of early 2016. The Fed has since been moderately successful in beginning to normalize policy. But even now remains accommodative according to its models. When in doubt, increase stimulus or delay rolling it back.

As many countries in the emerging world will attest, commodities are an easy route to growth. But it is notoriously difficult for central banks to spur economic activity in commodity driven economies when trouble hits. Much of this is due to the dominance of the US dollar in pricing commodities. Emerging economies have little control over the price of the commodities they export. Now that the party is over, commodity driven economies face difficult choices for monetary policies.

Without prudent fiscal policies during commodity price surges, it is difficult for emerging commodity economies to combat prolonged downturns. Since there is no ability to spur the principal driver of the economy, these countries have limited options to ride out a commodity bust. One of the tempting options is to lower interest rates and therefore weaken the domestic currency. By lowering the value of the domestic currency, the economy gains more of its own currency when the commodities are sold in dollars. And local revenues need not fall dramatically, even with commodity lower prices. There is a caveat, though. Weakening a currency typically leads to inflation and—in some cases—lots of it. Inflation can feed on itself and spiral out of control.

Why are central banks so loathe to allow inflation to fall or their economies to stumble? Because if they cannot accomplish their goals, they fail. And failure for a central bank is disastrous for an economy—particularly now. Loss of credibility and policy errors by central banks have always had consequences. And those costs are accentuated in an economic regime dominated by central banks.

This time around, however, central bankers have little ability to act counter-cyclically. Much of the emerging world is unable to stimulate its way out of a recession or slowdown, because the dollar is destiny and a stronger dollar is not a great destiny. The developed world will have a difficult time escaping monetary stimulus, because the fallout of "lifting off" is too much for most economies to handle. The US may be able to pull it off, but there is little indication that the ECB and BoJ are capable of doing it anytime soon. Central banks are trapped.

For the Fed, moving little can have as much impact as moving too far. Other central banks' actions complicate the Fed's decision due to the vulnerability of the US dollar to easing by developed country central banks. If the Fed tightens too much, the US economy could contract because of anything from the dollar to domestic credit conditions tightening too far. This convoluted math is the reality for modern monetary policy.

The unspoken truth is the Fed, the ECB, and certainly the BoJ have failed and consistently missed their inflation goals. All currently have loose policies to differing extents. Unfortunately for the emerging world, the US is the least loose, complicating their policy decisions. When central banks consistently fail to accomplish their mandates, it becomes dangerous for the global economy. There are few escape hatches for stimulus and loose policies when everyone is doing it. And it becomes all the more difficult to quit.

Even When You Say Nothing at All

The US Federal Reserve is rediscovering that talking—sometimes about doing nothing at all—can be a useful and powerful tool to transmit policy. With a strong dollar and slow global growth environment, the Fed was placed in a difficult spot at its March 2016 meeting. The FOMC was on a tightening path and projected it continuing apace. But financial conditions had become too tight too quickly. The Fed needed to loosen policy without losing credibility. Enter the forward guidance mechanism: guiding future policy without needing to make an explicit decision. And this is critical to the new policy making with little room to operate—the power of language (or lack thereof). While now well in the past, the March 2016 decision is the best example to date of the Fed using its forward guidance policy tool to control expectations.

First, the statement released after the Fed's March meeting indicated that members were refocused on global risks. Certainly, this is not the first instance of the Fed citing the global economy, but it reiterated a component of the Fed's decision-making mechanism that is difficult to monitor and only vaguely defined. Global risks are a permanent fixture of the economic landscape. This renders the ability to escape toward the dovishness of a global mandate an open-ended and powerful tool.

The policy statement was followed by a slew of Fed members giving speeches and interviews to clarify the message from the FOMC. A couple were hawkish, but Fed Chair Janet Yellen quelled those voices. Neither group clarified the weight the committee places on global uncertainty. They were aware of China's risk to the global economy with the potential to devalue its currency. But few, if any, had clarity on how much it matters to the Fed.

Speaking to the reasoning for the policy decision, Chicago Fed President Charles Evans emphasized the Fed's dual mandate as well as the global factor. Critically, "talk" did not stop with global uncertainty. Evans provided ample reason to be cautious on domestic employment and inflation. There are certainly reasons to be skeptical that the labor market mandate has been achieved. His concerns mirrored what his colleagues at the Fed, with a few exceptions, had stated.

On the employment side of the mandate, despite a US unemployment rate of 5%, there were reasons to doubt the United States was encroaching on full employment. Since the beginning of 2009, the labor force participation rate in the United States had declined from 65.7% to less than 63%. Alone, this represented 6.8 million people no longer in the labor force. Adding these workers back into the labor force would have increased the unemployment rate substantially, providing plenty of excuse for policy accommodation.

Narrowing the view, even the so-called "prime-age" workers participating in the labor force were under pressure (and remain) and had shown few signs of recovering. The prime-age worker data is used to strip out the effects of retirement, and there was (and is) significant room for improvement. But a longer-term view shows this decline is likely structural, not cyclical. Therefore, monetary policy may not be as effective at combating, never mind reversing, the trend.

Certainly, this is not a comprehensive review of the state of the labor market in early 2016, but it is indicative of the questions the Fed was (and in many cases still is) struggling to answer. And the reasonableness of its decision to walk back its pace of rate hikes.

Then and now, wages are often cited as a reason for the Fed to remain on hold. The Atlanta Fed's hourly wage tracker, by requiring earnings to be present in the current year and last, increases the likelihood of measuring the wage change for individuals constantly employed. This provides a better picture of wage growth in the United States than traditional indicators, given its measurement of constantly employed workers. But this too never recovered to prior levels following the most recent two recessions. This portends little inflationary pressure as wages are a link between the employment and inflation mandates.

Given that the Fed talked down the value of the dollar and expectations for future rate hikes, it provided some cushion to foreign exchange rates versus the dollar—regardless of the increasing divergence in policy. In talking about why it chose to do nothing, the Fed gently eased its policy stance while avoiding a loss of credibility. Not to mention the Fed later successfully reversed the talk and began to tighten policy again without losing credibility it retained.

The Battle for Wage Gains

The Fed's task is to maintain price stability and sustain maximum employment. It has enjoyed more success with the latter in recent days. Employment gains through mid-2017 are impressive, though given how far along in the labor cycle we are, the US economy may not produce those gains for long.

Participation in the labor force is near generational lows. Granted, this is partly due to retirement on one end of the age spectrum and greater education attainment on the other, but regardless of the reasons, fewer people are working. Although the usefulness and accuracy of the unemployment measure have been debated, unemployment is low and employment is growing at a steady clip. The relative health of the labor market has many policymakers at the Fed stating the United States is either at or near full employment. Full employment is synonymous with mission accomplished on maximum employment.

The Fed feels it has reached full employment. But it has set a relatively low bar for job creation to continue its tightening path. Gains above 125,000 are likely to suffice, meaning the Fed's policy path would be undeterred by a poor jobs report. This used to be the most important indicator for understanding the Fed's policy direction. But employment data are now somewhat of a nonevent. The release of the employment figures has not lost its relevance, but it has lost its spot as the driving force behind Fed decisions. This shifts the focus from employment data to inflation data. Inflation, the price stability portion of the mandate, has frustrated the Fed.

Inflation faces headwinds, most notably an aging population but also an increasingly services based economy, slow productivity growth, and large government debt overhang. Productivity growth may eventually pick up, but the demographics and services transition headwinds are long-tailed. And productivity has been stuck in a rut for a very long time.

With so many longer term forces weighing on inflation, the Fed will struggle to push inflation sustainably toward its 2% target. Elevated rents have also been of assistance for quite some time. This combination may allow the Fed a brief window to tighten policy and reduce its balance sheet.

However, to be able to fully normalize, the US economy will need to generate inflation and provide the Fed cover. (It should be noted that "normal" is the "after normal," and is not synonymous with historical averages.) This inflation increase will require consistent wage gains.

Suddenly, wages matter. They always have of course, but with employment hovering around "mission accomplished" territory and other inflation components like rent and energy already providing a lift, wages are the last game in town. Wage growth has been perpetually lackluster during the recovery.

The Fed can claim a small victory with a rise over 2016. Still, wage growth remains well below prerecession levels. For the health of the consumer, wage growth is likely the most important indicator of health in coming quarters and years. Without a sustained increase in wage gains, consumption is unlikely to trend much higher. If the US economy is going to accelerate, wages will need to do so first. This will—or should—be where the Fed refocuses its attention.

The rhetoric from the Fed feels oddly celebratory, as though the war with inflation and employment has already been won. The employment battle may have been, for now. But the war is far from over. The deflationary forces of boomer retirements will only accelerate from here. All eyes should be on wage growth. Remember, the ECB claimed victory in 2012—a laughable claim in retrospect. If the Fed claims victory in 2017, it may be remembered similarly.

And It's Losing

Following the recession in 2001–02, the US recovery saw few jobs gains, earning it the moniker "the jobless recovery." Certainly the US economy created jobs, but the number was mediocre. The economy grew, but the employment figures never seemed to keep pace. All recoveries have their disappointments. Unfortunately, the present recovery will be remembered in a similar vein, but the moniker may well be "the wageless recovery".

This is not to say that wages have not risen or will not in the future. But since the recovery began, wages have grown at a consistently slow pace, and this has been one of the more disappointing aspects of the recovery. Low-wage growth is not a recent development in the recovery. Instead, this has been a persistent feature of it. The issue is not declining wages but wage growth that has been consistently too low to generate the coveted quicker pace of economic growth.

On the surface, wage growth does not appear too bleak. In early 2017, the gains even appeared to have been accelerating. According to figures released monthly by the Bureau of Labor Statistics, average hourly earnings shifted to a quicker clip— from around 2% growth from 2013 to 2015 to more than 2.5% in early 2017. Without looking beneath the surface, those figures look reasonable.

But this is predominately a façade. After all, workers benefit from wages that rise more than inflation. This increases purchasing power and spurs consumption, driving economic growth. Not to mention wages outpacing inflation makes people feel richer, encouraging risk taking.

"Real" earnings—after stripping out the effect of inflation— have proven to be extremely tepid. Since the beginning of 2010, the average real wage gain has been a paltry 0.5%—far less than preferred.

Real wages are a product of wages and inflation. Higher real wages stemming from wage increases and steady inflation pressures are preferred and lead to the best growth outcomes. If wage growth continues to grow at its normal pace and inflation falls, real wages will rise. In this case, context matters.

In late 2014 and early 2015, oil prices collapsed and inflation followed. For the better part of 2014, inflation was growing at close to 2% from a year earlier. By early 2015, it was flat. Wages growth moved higher but only from a trend of 2% to 2.5%. This combination of near-zero inflation and higher wage growth pushed real wages to near 2%. The fastest clip of the recovery— by far.

The acceleration in wages from 2015 forward was the exception to the rules of this recovery. Real wages grew at their fastest clip of any point during the recovery but, driven predominately by falling inflation, not for all the correct reasons. At any rate, the pace was not maintained. Instead, inflation picked back up, and wage growth failed to accelerate.

There are consequences to a lack of real-wage growth. Granted, they are not as obvious as fewer jobs, but there are issues associated with consistently lower-wage growth. Consumer consumption accounts for more than 70% of the US economy. Additional spendable income is critical to growth. A healthier economy leads to more people being hired and (eventually) to a tighter labor market and increasing wages. It is a positive feedback loop—where one positive piece feeds another. But one piece appears to be broken.

Given the United States' heavy reliance on consumption for growth, the tepidness of the current wage pressures is disconcerting. During the rather lackluster growth of 2016, the contribution of consumption to GDP outpaced overall GDP growth in three out of four quarters. In other words, other lines were in aggregate detracting from growth. Consumption picked up the growth slack following the oil collapse and the subsequent decline in business investment.

In 2017, with unemployment at less than 5%, normally wage pressure would be expected, eventually followed by inflation pressures. The Fed would then be forced to tighten and so forth. This time is different. Wages have already failed to surge, and the question is not "when" but "will."

With inflation facing innumerable long-term headwinds, the Fed should consider paying much closer attention to wages and less to overshooting its inflation target. Without a sustained increase in real wage gains, consumption is unlikely to trend much higher. If the US economy is going to accelerate on a sustainable basis, then wages will need to do so as well. This will—or should—be where the Fed focuses its attention.

Even if the Fed attempts to target wage growth more, it will be nearly impossible for them to do so. Wages are more easily tackled from the auspices of fiscal policy. Many of these policies, including infrastructure spending and tax reform, are on the current administration's agenda. But a timeline is unclear.

Wages matter—especially in an economy so reliant on the consumer to drive its growth. Without real wage gains, workers and families fail to increase their purchasing power. Their incomes may increase, but their lifestyle does not.

The People's QE and Fed Creativity

There are a number of reasons maintaining credibility is critical. The need to use unconventional policies in the future is one of the leading concerns. Partly, QE can be difficult to defend, because—unlike the more traditional shifting of the fed funds rate—it works through transmission mechanisms that are hard to explain. Also problematic, QE, a powerful tool when used properly, becomes less and less effective the more it is used. In light of the diminution of QE's efficacy, central banks are taking note of an increasing chorus of creative—often conflicted—ideas for how they should execute monetary policy in the wake of global QE to combat the next downturn.

The leader of Britain's Labour Party, Jeremy Corbyn, has brought up the use of unconventional forms of QE. His "people's QE" (P-QE) is QE directly targeted at infrastructure investment. One benefit of P-QE is the less obscure and more visible effect on the economy. His plan would create an infrastructure bank and require the Bank of England to purchase debt issued by the newly formed bank. Instead of QE being ephemeral, it would now be a tangible policy for jump-starting an economy. Central bank intervention would become a more civic affair.

On the surface, Corbyn's plan is entirely reasonable. Economists become uneasy, though, when thinking about who would determine the size of the stimulus and how it would be administered. Traditionally, there is a separation of monetary and fiscal policy decisions. Responsibility for fiscal policy rests with politicians, and monetary policy is conducted by an independent board. This prevents short-term political goals from affecting long-term monetary policy. The suggestion that monetary policy directly facilitate fiscal policy violates this preferred dynamic. Or it did in the past.

But monetary and fiscal policy coordination is not a new concept. As mentioned, the US Congress has been contemplating a policy rule—basically a formula for setting key monetary policy rates. Last year, a group of Harvard economists including Larry Summers, pointed out that monetary and fiscal policy would be better off coordinated or—at least—not positioned to fight one another. And it makes sense. The US Treasury and Federal Reserve should not be working in opposition to one another (unintentionally) offsetting the benefits of each other's policies. The Harvard team found that the costs of the two fighting one another in the post-crisis era equated to roughly one-third of the Fed's easing effect on long-term rates.

The targeted P-QE is not entirely dissimilar from two recently executed QE strategies in the United States and China. Starting in November 2008, the Fed, in an effort to alleviate pressures in the system, purchased a substantial amount of mortgage-backed securities. This directly targeted a distressed asset class that had been pummeled in the Great Recession. The action was not coordinated with the Treasury and had no *direct* impact on employment. But it was targeted at a specific area of need.

China allowed local governments to exchange old distressed debt for new debt, extending maturities and pushing a potential problem down the road. Since much of this debt was issued to build infrastructure, the Chinese effectively executed the Corbyn plan but in a different order. Instead of issuing local debt, forcing the central bank to buy the local debt, and then building the infrastructure, the Chinese issued local debt, built infrastructure, and then had the central bank buy the local debt. Same basic steps, different order.

Corbyn's plan (and a recent slew of similar plans) is indicative a trend in the way politicians view monetary policy. But it is also how central bankers are forced to approach the monetary policy of the future: creatively. Creative monetary policy means Corbyn's suggestion may not sound so ludicrous in a few years. It may even sound reasonable. It also means that central bankers will continue to talk and write about monetary policy at near-zero interest rates and dream up new extensions of their current tools to try during the next slowdown. With government debt ratios too high to do much in the way of conventional fiscal spending, there will continue to be the temptation to use monetary policy to go on building and infrastructure sprees. It has even been suggested that tax breaks could be paid for with monetary policy. As long as the wall between monetary and fiscal policy stays up, these will remain suggestions.

Future QE will likely take on differing forms depending on the reason for the economic slowdown. And the glass wall between fiscal and monetary policy will be challenged, if not tacitly broken. With monetary policy becoming less effective on the margin, new tools are likely to be explored and called for by central banks, governments, and citizens. After QE, central bankers are learning to be creative. In the process, the rules that shaped traditional monetary policy may no longer be relevant.

The Anti-Volcker

For the Fed, the current economic situation is a mirror image of Paul Volcker's battle with inflation in the 1970s. When Volcker accepted the Fed chair from President Jimmy Carter in 1979, inflation was running rampant. In response, Volcker's Fed raised interest rates to levels never seen again. It is well known that he quelled inflation. But it is frequently forgotten how long it took to shake the specter of inflation. It took a very long time. And it took even longer to convince the public that inflation would stay at reasonable levels.

There are multitudes of reasons inflation ran rampant in the 1970s. Oil demand was growing at a time when the OPEC countries had significant power over the oil market and, therefore, prices. President Richard Nixon's decision to send Israel money to finance the Yom Kippur war and his choice to devalue the US dollar precipitated the first oil shock of 1973 and 1974. The breakdown of Bretton Woods (along with the value of the dollar) also contributed. After a slight reprieve, the second oil shock of 1978 to 1979 sent energy prices and inflation soaring again.

Oil and food were not the only culprits. The index tracking rent was growing by more than 12% a year in June 1980. A host of factors came together to dramatically escalate inflation and keep it at elevated levels. As Volcker learned, once inflation expectations become ingrained, they are hard to dislodge.

Over the next 30 years, the Fed kept inflation expectations under control. Researchers from the Federal Reserve Bank of New York built an inflation expectations model that covers that entire time period. Of note, their model suggests that inflation expectations peaked nearly a year after CPI peaked, then retreated only to resurge in 1984—nearly a decade after President Gerald Ford began his "Whip Inflation Now" campaign. Contrary to the popular narrative, the inflation war lasted well into the 1980s. And even then, the work suggests inflation expectations were hovering around 6% in the early 1990s.

As a consequence of his campaign to crush inflation, Volcker's Fed also depressed economic activity and threw the US into recession. Granted, Volcker's task was made more difficult by the near decade the United States had spent with elevated inflation prior to his becoming chair. The 1973–1974 oil shock had thrown the United States into a recession, leaving then-Chair Arthur Burns with a difficult choice. He had to decide between raising rates to combat inflation or lowering rates to fight unemployment. Burns choose to ease. Volcker, faced with a similar situation, acted decisively in the opposite direction. Burns' incompetence, miscalculation, or both likely contributed to the embedded inflation expectations that Volcker inherited.

There are several reflections of the 1970s inflation shocks in the present situation. For instance, oil is again a variable in the equation, as falling prices have pressured expectations for inflation downward. The United States' tepid recovery and booming oil production created a scenario in which the once dominant Middle Eastern producers were forced to push prices down, not up, to maintain their market shares. Instead of the strong global growth seen in the 1970s, today's global growth is tepid. Inflation expectations, worryingly high back then, are worryingly low today.

Likewise, policy missteps in the most important growth regions are again causing a certain amount of angst. In the 1970s, the US was the most important driver of global growth. Now this mantle belongs to China, whose 2015 decision to devalue its currency sent ripples through global asset markets and created global economic uncertainty.

All this leads to the challenge of setting Fed policy today. Raising rates too quickly and choking off any nascent inflation could set inflation expectations too low for the US economy.

But the comparison goes beyond the relatively simple task of not messing up inflation expectations. Oil alone did not cause problems in the 1970s, and it would be dangerous to forget the shocks that a significant currency devaluation can cause. The Fed must avoid causing a shock from a potential devaluation of the Chinese yuan. Granted, a yuan devaluation is not as consequential as the dissolution of Bretton Woods. Still, it could have deflationary ripple effects for the US.

Deflation is dangerous. In part because it causes interest payments on debt to grow as a portion of a borrower's income, making payments more difficult to cover. This is the primary reason the Fed should be so concerned about wages and inflation being so low. With the US awash in debt, wage deflation would be a spectacularly poor outcome for the US economy.

Unlike the 1970s, unemployment and inflation are low, and the US economy is in the midst of one of the longest recoveries in history. Now the Fed stammers in its attempts to increase rates with inflation stubbornly low and inflation expectations even falling. If it fails to push expectations higher—and keep them there—it may face an even more daunting task down the road. In essence, the Fed may be heading for its anti-Volcker moment.

Take It on Faith

One way or another, the Fed's policy path will be remembered as a comedy of errors. It always is. By so consistently telegraphing interest rate hikes and normalization, the Fed is backed into a corner. It may be a policy error to tighten to neutral, but backing away from higher rates could spark a crisis of confidence. That would be even worse. If the Fed commits a policy error, the error may be the best possible outcome.

The oddity of the Fed's position is the near guarantee that it will make a policy error. With little in the way of inflation and a nascent rebound in wages continuing to lag prior recoveries, the Fed has committed itself to "normalizing" interest rates toward a neutral policy stance. Precious little inflation pressure is appearing and economic growth remains anemic.

The Fed has cited the aforementioned as reasons for its slow and gradual approach to the process of tightening policy. Fed presidents frequently reiterate the primacy of data dependency in their process to determine policy while emphasizing the lack of a preset course for future policy. But the language is typically unidirectional—always focused on what data is needed to justify the preferred path. No one talks about what would constitute evidence for a reversal. And this creates complications for the Fed's ability to prudently conduct both present and future monetary policy.

The reasoning to normalize policy is "it must be done" not "it needs to be done." The logic as to why the Fed must remain on a tightening path is that it cannot afford to lose credibility (or create an obvious asset bubble). By committing the policy error of misreading the economy and significantly slowing an economic expansion, the Fed risks less credibility than it would by backtracking on it policy path. The Fed must maintain faith in the execution of its commitments and policies.

A commonly cited reason for the normalization of policy is that it will provide the Fed with room to be accommodative during the next downturn. Normalization will restore its ability to use the traditional stimulus measure of managing (lowering) the fed funds rate. The fear is that, unless rates can be raised to a level sufficient to give the Fed some firepower, it will be forced to return to unconventional policies.

The curious part about the campaign to move rates higher is that regardless of how close to "normal" the Fed gets, it will more than likely be forced to go to an unconventional policy to combat any downturn. The first step toward saving credibility might be to admit that extraordinary accommodation is now normal.

Unconventional policy relies heavily on Fed credibility. Credibility allows the Fed to commit to achieving a certain outcome and have markets believe it will happen. It keeps markets calm. Whether the policy is post-financial crisis QE, the manipulation of the entire yield curve in the 1940s and 1950s, or even the relatively mundane practice of forward guidance—all rely on markets believing in the Fed's future conduct. At this point, the fed funds rate will rise to a level sufficient to combat a slowdown. Unconventional policy is likely to be used to combat the next several downturns and become a far more regularly used tool.

Since the 1970s, the Fed has tightened around 3.5% to 4% per tightening cycle but loosened policy by more than 5% subsequently. With a current mid-point of only 1.125% for the fed funds rate, in order to gain enough room to lower rates sufficiently before reaching zero again, the Fed will be forced to tighten more than it currently projects.

If on the other hand the Fed continues to back away from its stated objectives, gaining back the trust of the markets will be difficult. In early 2016, the Fed slowly backtracked from its previous tightening path. Much of this was due to the strength of the US dollar, the potential for additional shocks from China, and negative interest rates in much of the rest of the developed world. This was good policy. It has helped the US economy to stabilize. The dollar declined, and inflation expectations rose. But the Fed cannot use this method of backing away frequently, or it will run the risk of losing credibility. In the 1980s, Volcker was forced to claw back credibility for the Fed. It took him years to do so.

Consistently committing the error of raising rates without needing to would slow the US economy. But a policy error does not have to have tragic outcomes. Raising rates at a moderate pace is unlikely to cause a recession, but it will hinder the recovery for little reason. At the pace of the Fed's own dot plot, interest rates will rise on a trajectory that almost guarantees an error. But it is an error the Fed may need to commit. Regardless of whether the policies are good or bad, the Fed cannot risk its credibility. Credibility is critical to the efficacy of the tools it will use in the next downturn. If need be, the Fed must commit an error.

WHAT IS NEXT?

The Federal Reserve Funding Infrastructure?

Ever so quietly, the US government has discovered an excellent new funding source for its projects: the US Federal Reserve. The "Fixing America's Surface Transportation Act," passed in late 2015, draws against the surplus account at the Federal Reserve to fund road and highway construction and repairs. On the surface, this might appear to be an innocuous, even laudable, use of the Fed's surplus, which has swelled as a (positive) side effect of QE.

In fact, there are a couple of reasons Congress' incursion to the Fed's balance sheet is, at the very least, disconcerting. First, it sets a precedent for future forays into what could be considered the Fed's own capital cushion. And second, it begins to erode the barrier between fiscal and monetary policy, a barrier that is critical to the proper execution of monetary policy.

Already, the Fed remits its operating surplus to the US Treasury. Due to the Fed's expansion of its balance sheet, this has become a consequential sum, far more than the Fed has remitted in the past. Oddly though, it was not this revenue stream that Congress decided to divert. Instead, the decision was made to draw from a sort of rainy day fund—the account also used to pay dividends to Federal Reserve shareholders (member banks).

Banks joining the Fed system are required to pay into the system, and they receive dividends from the surplus account on their ownership stakes in the Federal Reserve. Typically, this figure was fixed at 6%, but for larger banks, this figure is now pegged per congressional decree to no more than the yield of the US 10-year Treasury note. It is this surplus account that Congress used to fund its transportation bill.

When monetary policy directly finances fiscal policy, it is what is commonly known as "helicopter money." Granted the amount—around $26 billion—is small this time. But for a Congress searching for money to spend, the Fed's easy money may be too tempting.

Congress may believe it has found the golden goose that gives them money with little to no consequence to coming back for more later. The Fed is generating significant returns from its holdings of securities. This has been a boon to the US Treasury. But this may not last forever. And wittingly or not, Congress has begun to spend funds that could be critical to reducing the Fed's balance sheet in the future.

The FOMC has stated it will begin to allow the balance sheet, currently expanded to $4.4 trillion dollars after QE, to shrink slowly beginning in late 2017. But the Fed's ability to shrink the balance sheet is reduced by the uncertainty of the size or sanctity of its capital cushion. As the Fed starts to step away from purchasing assets to maintain its balance sheet, interest rates may rise modestly. As interest rates rise, bond prices fall and the Fed may incur losses. However, given that the Fed does not plan to sell any bond, instead letting them mature. Any losses will not be realized. But there is little room for error, because following the congressional appropriation, the surplus will be quite thin.

The end result? Congress gets its helicopter money, and the US Treasury will likely continue to receive outsized remittances. But all of this comes at the cost of the Fed's independence being slowly chipped away.

Raise the Inflation Target and Then Ignore Inflation?

There seems to be some consternation at central banks and their proxy think tanks around the world. Granted, monetary policy has not helped spark the recoveries we have grown accustomed to experiencing in the postwar era. But the question of precisely how much more monetary policy is capable of accomplishing—beyond what it already has—remains largely unanswered.

With a string of plus or minus 2% growth years for the US economy, fewer in Europe, and little inflation pressure anywhere, central banks appear to be at risk of losing their "hard-earned credibility" (as St. Louis Fed President Bullard has referred to it). There is a necessary distinction here. While typically the fear is losing credibility to a surge of inflation, losing credibility due to persistently undershooting inflation is as relevant.

Now the issue is fleeting inflation pressures as the boomer boom wanes. Sure, there are pockets of inflation and price pressures as preferences shift between generations. Rising rents due to a pivot toward renting is one such area. But the Fed does not see the risk as being always to the upside. Oil and the dollar are likely to cause some intermittent inflationary spikes (as always) but only of a transitory nature.

The risk the Fed faces is asymmetrical. Plenty of tools exist—and are simple to initiate—to combat inflation. These include selling off the Fed's balance sheet, raising the fed funds rate, and others. But the Fed cannot seem to get inflation sustainably higher.

Fed Vice Chair Stanley Fischer once stated that the Fed's inflation target of 2% was "within hailing distance." This is disingenuous at best. The Fed has been so far off it inflation target—and for so long—that predicting a rise to 2% inflation was simply not credible (it turned out he was wrong). Not, as Fischer so slyly stated, simply bump up against it. Overshooting inflation would not be a disastrous outcome for the economy. Importantly, sustained higher inflation would allow the Fed to get farther off zero. And farther from zero means less unconventional policy down the road.

San Francisco Fed President John Williams remarked that explicitly raising the inflation target or targeting nominal GDP would be beneficial for the Fed. St. Louis Fed President Bullard, on the other hand, changed his entire framework for thinking about monetary policy. He believes we are in a regime with little ability to handle higher interest rates. Between the two of them, they paint a rather unpleasant picture of the United States' ability to work through future shocks.

Implicit in this suggestion is that the US economy is in both a low-growth and low-inflation mode. Underlying the argument for a higher inflation target is something that could spur inflation and growth back to levels deemed acceptable. The question is: How exactly is it possible to reinvigorate inflation?

Williams has provided one piece: Move to a higher inflation target and commit to it. But credibility issues may be raised. After all, the Fed has never made it sustainably to 2%. So how will it make it to 3% or 4%?

But this may be beside the point in why speaking about a higher inflation target is apropos at the moment. Allowing the inflation target to move higher is not a policy in itself. Instead, it signals the Fed is willing to allow something to happen. But it does not outline the path. There are however, a couple ways that a higher inflation target could be achieved: fiscal policy and helicopter money.

In the case that either approach is used, a higher inflation target means that the Fed will not fight the fiscal stimulus. The actual purpose of a higher inflation target may simply be a method of getting the most of a fiscal kick, a guarantee that the effects will be allowed to flow through to the economy without the Fed tightening to temper inflation pressures. Unlike the contractionary policy that accompanied the first few rounds of QE, the Fed would actually welcome fiscal investment inflationary pressures to flow through into the economy—since their primary firepower in QE was counteracted by contractionary fiscal conduct.

Part of the importance of this signal would be to allow market participants to anticipate the inflation pressures and react accordingly. With inflation moving sustainably higher, interest rates would eventually have to move to counteract a potential overshoot but at a much higher level. This would give the Fed and the economy plenty of room to run.

Low growth and stubbornly low interest rates require different thinking in the conduct of monetary policy. In the context of the current Fed conundrum—wishing for higher interest rates but having no route to the goal—allowing fiscal stimulus to inflate the economy may be the only way to accomplish the task without more unconventional intervention by the Fed. This is precisely the anti-Volcker mentality. There is plenty of reverse ammo to temper inflation but few tools to stoke it. Maybe Williams and Bullard are the anti-Volckers that the US needs.

At the 2016 Jackson Hole, Wyoming, meeting, there was a debate concerning how monetary policy should be undertaken and whether the current thought process should be revised. As mentioned, Williams stated that the Fed's 2% inflation target requires some rethinking and likely needs to be higher. His proposal revolves around whether to allow inflation to run above the standard 2% target or completely pivot policy benchmarking away from inflation targeting. The reasoning? The natural rate of interest has fallen to an exceedingly low level. Remember that this is the theoretical federal funds rate that neither heats nor cools the economy. In theory, a higher inflation target implies a higher long-run fed funds rate. Or at least a way to avoid being trapped at a near zero fed funds rate.

While this is a logical critique of the current thinking around monetary policy, it may be a difficult pill for many to swallow. This is because it doesn't jive with the thinking of the past several decades. Allowing inflation to rise beyond the 2% target—and do so intentionally—is anathema to the post-Volcker world.

But Williams should not be written off without a careful examination of his two primary critiques of current Fed policy. First, a low inflation target is not useful in a low interest rate environment. Second, fiscal policy should be more countercyclical. While these may not seem closely related, the combination of the two could have profound implications for US monetary policy.

Behind the Williams argument is a desire to reduce overall policy reliance on unconventional tools, as well as an implicit acknowledgement that, regardless of whether or not the inflation target is moved higher, unconventional policies will be used far more frequently than in the past. The primary benefit of raising the inflation target is that—eventually—it should allow the Fed a higher fed funds rate. This gives the Fed a first line of defense to combat future recessions and shocks and—ultimately—less unconventional tactics.

Williams' confession that the US is in a low interest rate regime is similar to the argument and framework built by Bullard. A onetime hawk, Bullard pivoted to a "regime-based" model that implies that the Fed should hike only slowly. In Bullard's framework, the current economic conditions are likely to persist in the US. Their arguments are by no means identical. But both point toward policy prescriptions of low interest rates over a longtime horizon.

With two Fed presidents vocally stating that monetary policy needs to be rethought (and in very dovish ways), it is worth noting that the topic of the conference was "Designing Resilient Monetary Policy Frameworks for the Future." The discussion was fortuitously timed. After all, with Williams and Bullard challenging the traditional thinking of modern monetary policy, the frameworks discussed were more nuanced and less traditional than those used in the past.

Both a weaker dollar and higher oil prices are likely to place upward pressure on inflation at some point (a reversal of the 2014 to 2016 regime). But it will be only a temporary phenomenon. By moving the inflation target higher, the Fed would allow for more absorption and less reaction to currency and oil shocks.

Changes to policy targets and style do not happen quickly. But if the trend is moving in the direction of Bullard and Williams, in response to future downturns, the Fed will absorb much higher inflation without worrying about the fallout. Simply, if the Fed adopts a significantly higher inflation target, it is implicitly—or explicitly—announcing interest rates will be persistently lower for much, much longer.

Challenge China and Protectionism?

One way or another, there will be an adjustment in the trade relationship with China in the coming years. But the transition and its mechanisms have been poorly articulated. There is little question the trade relationship is lopsided between the United States and China. But this does not mean that harsh rhetoric and a trade war are necessarily in the cards.

The relationship is critical to global trade and growth. With more than $500 billion in two-way trade, much of the benefit (in terms of exports) accrues to the Chinese economy. However, this appears set to change. With the Trump administration promising to alter the equation, bring manufacturing jobs back to the United States, and generally make America great again, the proverbial tide appears to be turning toward domestic waters. The question facing the economist is how the adjustment will affect the global economy.

The current thinking around the China adjustment is a misnomer, because the adjustments are not as simple as widely implied. One the more common accusations is that China cheated the rules of international trade by managing its currency, the renminbi, to artificially low levels. This is both true and mis-leading. China was culpable of manipulating its currency lower during the early years of the 21st century but has since moved toward propping it up. Though once true, it is now an irrelevant statement and a deflection from the broader issues facing American workers.

The Trump administration has made clear its intent, whether through tweets or presidential appointees. It will reverse the perceived tide of manufacturing fleeing to China. Calls for high tariffs and penalties for shifting domestic production offshore have been targeted directly at US and foreign businesses. This is more than a step in the direction of protectionism.

In a *Wall Street Journal* opinion piece, Martin Feldstein defended the use of a border tax to increase revenues for the United States and create a more level playing field. The theory is relatively simple. The government should tax goods coming into the United States and provide a tax credit for goods shipped abroad.

At first glance, according to Feldstein, it would make imports more expensive. This would drive up the cost and cause American consumers to pay more for foreign goods, as well as cause American goods to be cheaper abroad. However, what Feldstein failed to note was that the ultimate regulator of global commerce, the dollar, would rise in value to offset the additional tax on imports. This would (theoretically) equalize the cost of both imported and exported goods to their original levels.

One downside to using this taxation mechanism is that it does nothing to solve the trade differential issue. Nor does it rebalance the trade relationship with China. Another potentially ugly side of border adjustability is the reduction in global dollar purchasing power. The global economy is heavily dependent on the dollar and its value. After strengthening for the better part of three years (and taking a breather in 2017), a further move upward would harm global growth. Regardless of whether it maintained an overall price level, it would hurt the rest of the world's ability to afford US goods.

A curse of maintaining the reserve currency is that any monetary policy movements have far more of a wide-ranging effect on the global economy than they would otherwise. A border tax resulting in a higher dollar would have catastrophic effects for countries that issue dollar-denominated debt or rely on commodities.

But here is the kicker. The United States is struggling to keep up with shifts in manufacturing. Technology is proving to be far more of a defining factor for the US worker than politics and trade agreements. In a July 2016 paper from the Center for Strategic Research, entitled "Will Technological Convergence Reverse Globalization," author T.X. Hammes considered the possibility that technology could alter the manufacturing and economic landscape more than politics will. A government does not impose this "natural protectionism." Rather, it is an economic and financial necessity to compete. This implies the dynamic of shrinking globalization without needing to deal a significant blow to the US economy.

If protectionism is happening on its own, why risk causing a trade war and an economic downturn to save jobs under threat from a more powerful and less tangible power? A side effect of the inevitability of natural protectionism is rendering moot much of the current tough talk on areas that depend on trade and manufacturing.

While the new, more protectionist global economy may encourage businesses to shorten their supply chains and automate production closer to consumers, it will not happen instantly. Manufacturers will invest and pivot over time. Years will pass.

Globalization and the expansion of trade were tremendous benefits, both to the United States and to the global economy. But this is waning. Trade is not the panacea for developing-world growth that it once was. Nor is automated manufacturing a job boon for the developed world. It is not obvious who wins in the new naturally protectionist world. But regardless, the environment may be inevitable.

In the end, there are few easy remedies to the China puzzle. The tools used to fight a trade war are blunt instruments. The global economy would be caught in the crossfire between the US and China. If thought through in their implementation, a border tax could raise US federal tax revenue without too much spillover. But the spillover could also be immense, and it will need to be done with care.

"Protectionism" is a dirty word. It suggests an unwillingness to engage in the global economy. Economists believe it results in negative consequences for both the domestic and international market economies. In most cases, protectionism represents the conscious choice to keep a nation out of the international economy in order to avoid a particular negative outcome. Once mostly relegated to the political sector, protectionism has resurfaced in economic debates. And it may be an inevitable outcome of today's economy.

The current political rhetoric regarding trade is causing angst among economists and some political observers. If the politicians are being honest, trade policy is leaning heavily toward a protectionist mantra or at least a protectionist stance. This conjures an uneasy correlation to the United States' reactionary mentality in the 1930s. And rightfully, anything hearkening to those days generates fear.

Globally, protectionism is rampant and takes on a variety of forms. A locally sourced materials or manufacturing requirement in exchange for access to markets is one of the more popular forms in the modern economy. Brazil is the poster child for demanding local production.

The US is not moving in that direction rapidly. But there are calls for high tariffs and penalties for shifting domestic production offshore. There should be no misunderstanding. This is a step in the direction of protectionism.

Oddly, the time that protectionism would have proved most productive has passed. After all, the US economy is not reliant on manufacturing. Not to mention that, according to Boston Consulting Group, more manufacturers said they were likely to add capacity in the US rather than China in the next five years.

Politicians and market participants argue that policy will decide the fate of global connectivity. In fact, though, as mentioned above, technology is proving to be its defining characteristic.

Hammes' technological protectionism differs from the artificial, politically imposed type. Instead of forcing businesses to produce goods in the United States or be penalized, he suggests that modern production and supply chain needs will necessitate this shift toward a decline in globalism.

Extrapolating from Hammes, this is a "natural protectionism." Not imposed by a government, it is an economic and financial necessity to compete. This necessarily implies the dynamic of shrinking globalization without necessarily a significant blow to the US economy.

But it might also not be quite the benefit it once would have been. Even the imposition of natural protectionism may bring few manufacturing jobs back to the United States. The reality is twofold. First, the US is competitive due to automation, not labor costs. Most of the jobs will accrue to robots. Second, the new manufacturing jobs will not be similar to those that left. The jobs coming back will be concentrated in keeping the robots running and programming them correctly. This is not the same as the manufacturing jobs that left for China and elsewhere in terms of necessary skillset.

This leaves politicians and economists in a quandary. The slowing and possible reversal of globalization is supposed to be completely bad. And for some developing countries looking for a manufacturing edge with low labor costs, it will be. For the developed world though, it may simply be a positive.

A side effect of the inevitability of natural protectionism is rendering much of the current tough talk on trade and manufacturing locale moot. With the global and US economies moving in that direction, there is little need to attempt to force it through rhetoric, revocation of trade treaties, and retaliation for perceived economic damage.

Then again, there is a significant time differential. The new economy may encourage businesses to shorten their supply chains and automate production closer to consumers. And this is rightfully disconcerting to some. In a scenario where the United States sparks a trade war, the Peterson Institute for International Economics estimates substantial side effects to the US economy in terms of jobs and GDP. The Peterson Institute is probably correct in its assessment of the consequences in the near term of a pivot toward protectionism including substantial job losses in areas surrounding port cities (almost 90,000 in Houston alone in their "trade war" scenario). Again, the question for politicians to consider is: If protectionism is happening on its own, why risk causing an economic downturn to prove a point? There is none.

Trading for Protectionism?

The United States pulled out of the Trans-Pacific Partnership (TPP). Once considered the most ambitious free trade agreement in history, the TPP aimed to set the trajectory and tone of trade in Asia as a balance to a rising China. Now there is an economic vacuum to fill. For countries looking for partners in growth, China is the obvious choice.

The demise of the TPP will not affect near-term US growth, but many of the United States' staunchest Asian allies, including many that are in disputes with China, were among those negotiating the TPP. For those countries, including Vietnam, the economic gains and strategic alliance with the US were significant. The lack of TPP leaves them at a strategic disadvantage.

The TPP was a long-term investment in trade liberalization. Writing the rule of trade in Asia with a durable framework was a laudable goal. The problem was that the US would realize few immediate gains from striking the agreement. With the rhetoric of supposed job-flight in the aftermath of trade agreements firmly established, it is little wonder there is trepidation around trade.

The United States gambled that it could play a substantive role in setting the rules for Asian trade. If China and India had joined, it might have worked. The economic benefits could have been substantial, but only far down the road. But the US was too big to benefit from a deal involving too few real changes to the global economic regime.

US credibility in Asia—the most populous region in the world—was damaged, but the TPP will also hit much closer to home. Mexico and Canada joined the negotiations. Chile and Peru were involved as well. The US withdrawal not only throws away the potential for a trade agreement in Asia but also may cause countries that expended significant political capital for the TPP to retreat from free trade for the foreseeable future.

In response to the negotiation of TPP, China has been constructing its own trade framework in Asia and beyond. With the United States in retreat from Asia, the power in the negotiations for the Regional Comprehensive Economic Partnership (RCEP) shifts to China. While it is an ASEAN agreement, the dominant economic force in the negotiations will be China. Following a disintegration of the TPP, participants can turn to the RCEP and look to gain access to China and India. Neither country was included in the TPP. For Mexico and Canada, who have access to the United States through NAFTA—another agreement in limbo—this could be the preferred outcome. That's not something the Trump administration likely wants to contemplate. The remnants of US soft power in Asia are fading.

Lacking leadership, it is difficult to see where free trade goes from this juncture. A recent development in global trade is that the United States is not the only game in town. China's "One Belt, One Road" in many ways mimics the West's traditional methods of expanding its influence and economic system.

The abandonment of TPP also allows for a relaxation of the reforms the United States was pushing. US companies competing with state-owned enterprises (SOE) understand that these businesses do not typically have profit goals. They are far more frequently used to employ as many people as possible and push political agendas. This makes it difficult for profit-minded companies to compete. The TPP pushed for SOE reform. But now there is little reason to expect any imminent changes.

The demise of TPP suggests that prospects for the TTIP—the free trade deal between the US and EU—are not much better. The chances of completing the deal in the current economic and political climate are slim.

In Asia, TPP was probably second best to the RCEP anyway. The RCEP is a stunning undertaking. Not only is it outside of the sphere of US influence, but it includes China, India, South Korea, ASEAN-5, Australia, and New Zealand, among others. In terms of global growth, the RCEP is the center of it.

What happened to the TPP is disturbing not because of what it will do to the US economy. But it sets the tone and precedent that the United States is not going to be the center of trade or economics. Any future deals will lean more in favor of the United States or not be negotiated or consummated at all. US trade is in retreat, and so is its influence.

Get Ever More Creative?

With trade unlikely to be the savior in the after normal economy, the attention will likely shift back towards central banks, and their ever more creative policy. To this point, the Bank of Japan

(BoJ) must have felt the pressure to shift its policy direction and implementation shifting to an entirely new level of stimulus. It certainly delivered when it announced yield curve targeting in 2016.

The BoJ has always been creative. But the BoJ stepped away from its previous method of implementing quantitative easing and shifted its focus to "yield-curve targeting." This sounds far more complicated than it really is. In essence, the BoJ committed to maintaining the 10-year yield on Japanese government debt at 0%. Doing so requires the continuation of government bond purchases, except now executed in a more objectively oriented manner.

In guidance regarding the length of the newly announced easing, the BoJ made it clear that they would do so until inflation rises sustainably above its 2% target. Critically, this removed the previous methodology of expanding the monetary base (printing money) by a specific target per year, replacing it with a more flexible framework. If there is little upward pressure on yields, a lower amount of bond purchases will be needed. If upward pressure begins to emerge, the purchases would increase.

In practice, this means that the BoJ is now controlling the entire yield curve. But the BoJ went farther in its policy revamp by committing to focus on the yield curve until the Japanese economy overshoots its inflation target. The notion of allowing inflation to overshoot its target is somewhat akin to increasing the inflation target itself. This makes the inflation target gambit one of the more—if the not the most—interesting elements to the policy reboot.

Why? Few economists believe the BoJ will reach a sustainable level of 2% inflation any time soon (if ever). This implies the BoJ quietly but intentionally extended its QE *indefinitely*. There is no explicit end date and no simple path to sustainable 2% inflation.

The BoJ stated it would attempt to push observed inflation above 2% "at the earliest possible time." The design is an effort to increase expectations for inflation and break the ingrained deflationary mindset in Japan. By using "observed inflation," the BoJ indicated it wants to see prices rise. It does not merely want to expect it.

Will yield-curve targeting work? If history is any guide, yes. Or at least it is a sustainable proposition. Even the United States has experience with targeting the yield curve. The Fed did so as the country emerged from World War II. It effectively capped rates for the better part of a decade. In the US experience, yields did not breach the yield curve targets, and there were few hiccups in the execution of the strategy. Essentially, the BoJ is taking a page from the Fed's playbook that is more than a half-century old.

This should assuage the fear that the BoJ was out of bullets. Since it is now explicitly targeting the yield curve, the options for additional stimulus range across the yield curve. It could lower the short-term rate to be more negative. Or it could lower the long end of the curve. Or it could do both. In essence, the BoJ now has the entire curve to explicitly manipulate and can do so quickly.

There are certainly risks. As one dissenting vote stated, the bank may actually need to accelerate its government bond purchases. It is true that the strategy may cause the BoJ to expand the monetary base more quickly. In terms of accomplishing its greater-than-2% inflation target, this may not be an adverse scenario.

Another rebel vote was concerned about the commitment to overshoot inflation, stating that it was not a realistic target. *This is probably true.* The unrealistic nature of the target was likely part of the point. It hinted at the near perpetuity of the easing without explicitly stating it.

Monetary stimulus in Japan is not going anywhere. The BoJ broke new ground for the current easing cycle by committing to target the yield curve and overshoot its inflation target. This may inspire other central banks to try similar tactics, during the next downturn. The BoJ has committed to undertaking monetary stimulus for a very, very long time. Japan's perpetual easing has only just begun.

The Last Chance: Trumponomics?

As we enter the era of Trumponomics, it is important to understand the difference between a well-articulated, -constructed, and -executed fiscal stimulus and a poorly designed one. While there is little chance anything substantial will pass in the current political environment, fiscal measures may become popular methods of stimulating the after normal economy.

Understanding where the economy sits is critical to getting the most bang for the added deficit buck. Unemployment is low, and the economy has not seen a recession in seven years. Meanwhile, monetary policy is tightening albeit from exceedingly accommodative levels. This dampens some of the potential benefits. Simply, the US economy now stands in a different place than is usually the case during the potential introduction of the typical fiscal package.

It is tempting to draw parallels. But substantial differences exist between the current economic environment and the era of Reaganomics. In 1981, the United States fell into a recession. After seven years of expansion, it is debatable whether the United States is due for a recession soon. In an attempt to increase the size of their toolkit, the Fed is tightening monetary policy to combat the next recession, whenever it might be. President Reagan entered office after Volcker broke inflation and fed funds were (for the most part) declining. The US dollar hit a half-century peak in 1985 and proceeded to devalue rapidly in response to the 1985 Plaza Accord. This was an added tailwind to policies implemented.

There is little question the Fed will be tightening in 2017 and 2018 (barring a recession). At least to some degree, this will undoubtedly dilute the overall impact of any stimulus package. The Trump administration will need to confront this reality.

The US economy is not in crisis mode. It is not growing as quickly as it was in the 1990s, and participation in the labor force is declining. This is also not the time of Reagan, when similar policy ideas were implemented. The boomers are on their way out and no longer the economic catalysts they once were. To a degree, this limits the effectiveness of infrastructure spending on employment. Boomers may not come back to participate in such a program.

President Trump's $1 trillion infrastructure proposal could be substantial (even if it is funded with tax credits), but there are hurdles. For instance, the United States already passed a $300 billion infrastructure bill in early 2016. This was a smaller package than the plan's original $478 billion. The possibility of a package more than three times that size seems tenuous.

Furthermore, with US economic expansion well under way, it makes little sense to undertake an infrastructure plan. Infrastructure investment would have a direct employment benefit, and the US economy will require it more earnestly during the next recession than it does now.

The possible inability to push through an infrastructure package may be a good thing. Research findings consistently suggest that infrastructure spending is less stimulative than tax cuts. Alberto Alesina and Silva Ardagna, in a study spanning nearly 40 years of fiscal adjustments across developed economies, find fiscal stimulus done through tax cuts and paid for by spending cuts to be the most effective method of having a two-pronged, longer-term stimulus package that could effectively reinvigorate some demand and inflation for a time.

This may seem intuitive, but perhaps even more important is the timing and promotion of a fiscal package.

This is because the type of tax cuts and delivery matters. Not all tax cuts will stimulate in the same manner. Infrastructure spending, direct payments, and tax cuts elicit different reactions depending on how they are packaged and delivered. The size of payments, their frequency, and the permanence and length of policy shifts also play into the effectiveness of a stimulus. Cutting taxes and having the outcome be effective at stimulating economic growth is not as simple as it might seem.

The importance of intentional design and delivery comes from the work of Richard Thaler and his theory of mental accounting. The basic thrust of the theory, as applied to stimulus packages, is that people react differently to different sized stimuli. A large sum is more likely to be considered an asset, and smaller amounts treated as income. A study by Graziani, van der Klaauw, and Zafar found that when people considered the "lump sum" of the 2011 payroll tax cut, they intended to spend 10%–18% of it. But after it was doled out in pieces, they spent far more: 28%–43%. Mental accounting matters.

For individuals, incremental, small pieces are more likely to be considered income and less likely to be saved or used to pay down debt. Lump sums or a dramatic drop in marginal rates may not be the most effective route. In other words, a shock amount would be less effective than a steady increase. As politicians consider designing a new tax policy, they must keep this in mind.

If the Trump tax proposals were unaltered, it would result in a significant drop in rates. If the new administration wants maximum effectiveness, it should slowly and steadily phase in the new, lower tax rates. Done all at once, the tax cuts may not be as successful as they could be otherwise.

One reason the phase-in may be worth considering is the amount of reduction on the higher income tax brackets. While the percentage decrease declines at the top, the dollar amounts will be much larger. The likelihood is consumers will treat these windfalls as assets instead of as income. And if spent, those larger upper bracket tax cuts could be a primary driver of a successfully implemented plan.

By implementing the tax cuts through a step-down—say 25% of the total per year, the digestion may feel more like income than an asset. With about $1 trillion of expected budgetary impact, the implementation of personal income tax policy will be critical to the overall success or failure of Trumponomics. Yes, corporate tax policy is important as well, but the loopholes make it difficult to assess. This also makes it hard to determine increases to potential growth.

The United States cannot afford to have tax cuts and infrastructure spending that do not generate substantial benefits. The deficits and resulting debt will simply become too burdensome over time. This will further reduce growth in the future. Slow and steady cuts are the best path to making America spend again.

Another reason it is critical to do the tax cuts well is because of the Fed. The Fed has shifted its stance. It has ever so gently pivoted from data dependent to Trump dependent. Until now, the post-crisis Fed has claimed to be data dependent in its policy making process. But waiting for the data to justify tighter monetary policy has been an arduous, painful process. It took three rounds of QE and years of persistently low rates to maintain the economic recovery. Even then, the Fed has been forced to step back from its tightening policy a number of times. This time may be different, however. Now it has the promise and perils of Trumponomics.

In the past, when the Fed attempted to tighten policy, it was forced to step back. Whether driven to do so by a shock from China or a slowing in the US economy, those shifts were data driven: shocks or potential shocks to inflation or employment. For a moment, the Fed seems to be deemphasizing its self-imposed data-driven mandate in favor of a new dependency: a Trumponomics dependent policy rule.

There were signs of the shift. Some Fed officials made it clear that they had already included in their assumptions and projections some of the anticipated economic effects from a shift in fiscal policies. Many of the Trump administration's policies would create economic outcomes that would affect or potentially affect the path of monetary policy.

Granted, the Fed could fall back on its tried-and-true position of data dependence. But this would be counterproductive. Fed officials made it abundantly clear that it would like to increase interest rates in order to have policy ammo to combat the next economic downturn. They now seemed to have the cover.

This pivot creates a far more interesting policy framework from the Fed. The pivot to Trumponomic sentiment from data becomes intriguing and critically important in understanding the potential for the Fed to be proactive to fiscal and other economic policies out of Washington, DC.

This proactive mindset differs from the data-driven reactionary style of policy delivered over the past several years. Significant inflation pressures were expected to materialize before the Fed reacted. Now the expectation of a policy shift in Washington is affecting the delivery of monetary policy with little if any detail on the fiscal policies that will be implemented.

And the sentiment—the feeling—is that things are getting better and the economy will positively react to tax cuts and infrastructure spending. These policies will push inflation and wages higher, and employment gains will continue. In other words, the Fed will need to react to balance its dual mandate of price stability and employment. With its stance, instead of waiting for the data to react, the Fed will have already done so.

Within this new framework, how does the Fed provide the market with legitimate guideposts for anticipating the unfolding of monetary policy? If the Fed has converted from reacting to economic variables and outcomes to policy ones, then it will be difficult for it give meaningful guidance about its intended rate path. The efficacy of forward guidance has been lackluster at best. Still, there is certainly some usefulness. It creates a sense of stability in the Fed's path. While the path may change, there is a certain coherence in the forward projection, albeit typically incorrect.

A primary example of the rapidity of a shift in the Fed's thinking is illustrated by the decision to raise interest rates in March 2017. With only a couple of weeks remaining before the decision, the Fed had spent little time preparing the markets for a rate hike. With sentiment pointing to a buoyant second half of the year, the Fed shifted its stance quickly.

There are caveats to the Fed's stance. Seemingly overlooked in the Fed's math is the amount of uncertainty surrounding the actual policy outcomes. There is considerable uncertainty in predicting and projecting economic data. But policy outcomes are also highly uncertain and subject to change. Whether it is in the tax plan, a limitation in the infrastructure bill, or both, there is likely to be disappointment. Given a fiscal policy dependent Fed, the trajectory of monetary and fiscal policy are now closely—perhaps too closely—tied.

This creates a problem for Fed independence. Not in the sense of Congress dictating what the Fed's policy should be, but very much in the sense of congressional actions having a direct impact on the direction of monetary policy. Any time there is a causal relationship between fiscal and monetary policy, it should make people nervous.

But these policies are far from a given. Some may not be positive from the Fed's point of view. Tax and regulatory changes will boost growth (and likely spark some inflation), but a border-adjusted tax could cause the dollar to unduly strengthen. How are Fed officials including these not so positive potential outcomes in their assumptions?

How would the Fed likely react to a disappointing fiscal package? It would likely force the Fed to readopt a relatively dovish stance similar to the retreats seen in the wake of data disappointments. This has consequences in and of itself. Delays and disappointments in the Trump administration's fiscal stimulus and tax policies now have monetary policy consequences.

This is not a positive. Raising rates in anticipation of the introduction of policies explicitly intended to accelerate growth runs the risk of the Fed becoming quickly and overtly politicized. It also increases the chance of policy mistakes.

The problem with the Fed's pivot from data driven to Trumponomics driven is the lack of clarity. Expectations can differ wildly concerning the outcomes of known fiscal policies, never mind ones that are unknown. They can also be delayed, pushing out the timeframe frame for an already impatient Fed. The Fed should have stuck to its policy of data dependence, but it may be too late for that now. Even the Fed was swept off its feet by Trumponomics.

And this may prove a difficult position for the Fed. For eight years of on-and-off QE, the Fed held the undivided attention of markets. Now the Republican Party (GOP) is in power. And its long-heralded initiatives of repealing the Affordable Care Act, reforming the tax code, scaling back regulations, and incentivizing infrastructure spending have been cheered by markets that needed a new narrative.

But markets overestimated the speed with which change would come to Washington, DC. Indeed, much of the post-election "Trump bump" dissipated rapidly. The US dollar surged following the election. But then fell back to its pre-election levels. Inflation expectations rose on the assumption that infrastructure spending would stoke upward pricing pressures. These also declined. Expectations for tax reform are slowly became expectations for tax breaks—and potentially temporary ones. From a quick, first glance it seems as though the entire Trump agenda was swiftly written off—as though the chaos in Washington will derail it all.

This is simply not the case, though certainly some of the enthusiasm surrounding the plans has been reduced. Nor is it necessarily a bad thing that some of the hype was drained from the system. The GOP and Trump always had similar priorities but differing specifics. Trump's team is less concerned with budget deficits than getting a significant tax cut. Many GOP members in the House and Senate feel the opposite.

The healthcare, tax, and infrastructure initiatives always required complicated and intricate political maneuvering. They will all require a diverse (or divided) GOP to vote as a bloc. This will further reduce the certainty of any outcome. In contrast, regulation can be reduced substantially by executive order, and President Trump has utilized these with frequency. This means there are fewer barriers to that portion of the agenda. A lack of clarity over which agenda (and how much of it) will eventually pass and what the timeline will be keeps markets guessing.

Tax and infrastructure are of the utmost importance. Lower taxes equals better profits. Better profits (all else equal) means valuations increase. That is unequivocally positive for markets. In a similar vein, infrastructure spending would be expected to spur inflation pressures, and inflation pressures have a direct impact on the price the US government pays on debt (since interest rate would likely rise).

Fiscal policies will always have detractors. The nearly instant reaction of global markets leaves little room to doubt their market impact. One of the campaign promises economists feared most, the renegotiation of NAFTA, does not appear to be anything other than a modernization project. This could be nothing to fear, though we are months away from understanding the exact nature of the negotiations.

And that is what is causing the tremendous amount of heartburn for markets: the timeline. For investors, watching the tax and infrastructure initiatives get pushed farther and farther out is accentuating the uncertainty already presented by a lack of clarity on the details.

With the legislative branch distracted, markets are left with little guidance in terms of either timelines or outlines. That is the reason that markets react to happenings in Washington. Not because there is a direct, negative linkage to the US economy but because it dramatically slows the process of the policies markets want.

Without some policy victories, markets may be forced to refocus on the Federal Reserve. The Fed itself is unlikely to greet this warmly. As previously stated, many of the Fed's members have openly admitted to including fiscal policies into the economic projections they use to recommend monetary policy. In other words, the timing matters—not only for markets—but also for the evolution of the Fed's monetary policy stance.

Fed, however, may well be tired of talking its way back from a rate hike path. "Good enough" growth may prove "good enough" for a Fed desperately wanting to normalize toward neutral. Markets and the Fed are indirectly but inextricably linked to the happenings in Washington. The evolution of politics in Washington will have a direct and uncomfortable influence on both.

Because of the low inflation pressures and delays in policy from Washington DC, Minneapolis Fed President Neel Kashkari warned that the Fed was at risk of making a 1970's style mistake— only in reverse. Whereas the Fed of forty years ago was too slow to raise rates in response to high inflation, Kashkari's idea is that, with both inflation expectations and realized inflation now declining, today's Fed should rethink (i.e. lower) the trajectory of its policy tightening. This is a sort of "anti-Volcker" moment for the Fed dissenters.

For the past several years, the Fed has serially missed its 2% inflation target, and (the argument goes) the Fed needs to be truly committed to its target, or it will lose credibility. Already, the Fed has to explain the deviation.

In the same meeting Kashkari stated the Fed was making a mistake, Fed Chair Janet Yellen expressed confidence in the eventuality of hitting 2% inflation. This was only moments before stating that the Fed would look through the current weak inflation figures. While somewhat unexpected in its directness, Yellen's statement is less than shocking. This Fed frequently sees oil as having only a transitory impact on inflation and takes care to avoid placing too much credence in subsequent readings. In other words, choosing to call sharp, one-time movements in prices transitory is far from abnormal.

In its determination to continue removing accommodation, the Yellen Fed is attempting to avoid the Greenspan trap, meaning it wants to avoid keeping rates too low for too long which could create unwieldy bubbles, as the Greenspan Fed did with housing. In the process, today's Fed is attempting to give itself ammunition for future downturns in economic activity, and not be caught off guard by Trump administration stimulus. The indication here is that the Fed's reaction function—how it respond to US economic developments—has shifted toward a macroprudential framework, this being a sort of "do no harm" style of monetary policy that seeks to avoid building bubbles while not slowing the economy too much.

That sounds a lot like the definition of the natural, or neutral rate of interest. The natural rate of interest is the interest rate of "do no harm but do no good" that should neither accelerate nor decelerate the economy. Theoretically, after reaching this neutral zone inflation should be in the 2% area (emphasis on theoretically). At the moment, the U.S. nominal neutral fed funds would be near 1.5–1.75% depending on inflation.

This is where the Fed wants to be, and it is not too far from where we are currently. The primary danger to the natural rate standard now is the downward trajectory of inflation. If it keeps falling, the Fed could overshoot neutral and accidentally tighten policy before it intends to do so.

This point of view is radically different from the anti-Volcker sentiment of 2% inflation at any cost. At issue is the supremacy of price stability, which the Fed believes is synonymous with inflation of around 2%, and which is, after all, part of the Fed's official mandate (a claim that macroprudential policy cannot make).

Despite the logic of the anti-Volcker argument, it is likely to lose out to the macroprudential framework for a few reasons. Those on the Fed fearful of falling into the Greenspan trap believe interest rates can get to neutral and not prevent medium-term inflation from getting to 2%. This eliminates part of the argument for the anti-Volcker crowd, who suggest that continued rate hikes could squelch inflation.

Second, the Fed is wary of being blamed for the next bubble. By moving toward neutral, there may be some cover. Lastly, the Fed needs to reload its policy arsenal. There needs to be something other than the balance sheet to combat the next downturn. Otherwise, it risks further calls to increase oversight. These three considerations are likely to outweigh the lackluster inflation readings in the near-term in dictating inflation pressure.

Another factor at play is the changing of the guard next year at the Fed. Without knowing who will be there and for how long, the current Federal Open Market Committee may want to have a balance sheet reduction policy in place before their successors take office. This dynamic may be far more important over the next six months than many market and Fed watchers think.

For the moment, it appears avoiding the Greenspan trap is more important to understanding the Fed's path than the anti-Volcker's. But neither side is likely to stand down quietly. In other words, even if Trumponomics does not deliver on growth, the Fed will deliver on rate hikes.

Reloading the Fed's Gun?

If the Federal Reserve's recent rhetoric is to be believed, we are in the twilight of its Great Recession intervention. In the midst of the crisis, the Fed bought up assets in what was called an "unconventional" monetary policy maneuver. These purchases eventually exceeded $4 trillion. To maintain this stimulus, the Fed promised not to shrink its stockpile—at least for a long, long time. That time has apparently arrived now. Some commentators fear the potential fallout. But there is little reason to fear.

It is a misnomer to refer to QE as "unconventional." Central banks have long used it, or other policies that use their balance sheets to buy assets, to achieve monetary policy objectives. The Fed did so during the Great Depression, to cap yields on US debt following World War II and to undertake "Operation Twist" during the Kennedy administration. And the Fed is not alone in its use of these unconventional policies. Nordic countries did so in the 1990s. The Bank of Japan (BoJ) purchases a wide variety of assets regularly. The fact of the matter is that these tactics have been used often with varying degrees of success.

Granted, before the 1980s and 1990s, central bank asset purchases were predominantly used to finance government deficits during wartime. The reasons for doing so are now centered on combatting financial crises and boosting aggregate demand. The reasons for asset purchases and unconventional policies have drifted, but using them is not a new policy tactic.

The Japanese experience is commonly cited as a failure to escape these not-so-unconventional policies. But there are also examples of effective use and unwind. In the early 1990s Sweden successfully undertook an unconventional policy before unwinding it. It is also forgotten that the BoJ was unwinding its own. It was the onset of the Great Recession that caused Japan to reverse course—a case of impeccably poor timing.

Central banks typically unwind these policies over a long period. For the Fed, it will be a prolonged process. Notably, if history is any guide, the unwinding has not been too disruptive to economic growth—only minor drags on economic growth and inflation. Granted, the sheer size of the Fed's purchases may test these findings.

One worry is that the end of these policies will cause long-term bond yields to spike. The Fed's purchases reduced the "term premium." This is the compensation to an investor for taking the risk of buying a longer-term bond. It pushes yields lower. But as it stands, the stimulative impact of the balance sheet on bond yields has already been waning. And as the Fed continues to hold those assets, the impact will continue to fall.

Inflation, and the threat of it rising, is the primary risk an investor is compensated for through the term premium. This is why, as the Fed backs away, the term premium—and therefore longer-term bond yields—will be even more closely tied to inflation and inflation expectations (specifically shocks to it).

It is therefore worth noting that inflation is not a threat. Not to mention that the Fed is raising short-term interest rates and the US economy is not accelerating. In a way, this is an optimal backdrop to roll off the final remnants of crisis era monetary policy. Not because the US economy is accelerating. Somewhat just the opposite. With inflation pressures tenuous and monetary policy tightening, yields on longer-term debt are unlikely to shoot higher.

A few developments could alter the equation. The Trump administration's slowly delivered regulatory relief and promised tax reform would change the math by spurring economic growth and stoking inflation pressures. There is some probability these will materialize. But it is difficult to make a proper assessment of the policies without the details. And they may still be a long way off.

For the past century, QE style unconventional policies have been a tool for central banks. This will not change and—more likely—is becoming a staple of US and developed world monetary policy. During the next recession, it will either be used or threatened again. By reducing the amount of assets—mostly mortgages and US government debt—the Fed regains its capacity for the next time it needs to stimulate the economy.

And with the effects of QE quickly waning anyhow, there should be little direct effect on growth and inflation from removing its final vestiges. There could be some unique problems in the mortgage market as the Fed ceases to be the largest buyer, but some pains are inevitable.

As it all ends, it is not a given that longer-term yields will rise. That fear is overblown. Inflation is what truly matters. And there are few reasons to believe that tightening monetary policy will do anything other than push those expectations lower, keeping longer term yields in check. It is time to stop worrying.

BEYOND AFTER NORMAL

Commentators proclaiming a "new normal" for the global economy have been steady. And it is true that the economic framework for the United States, and the trajectory of the global economy, is different than that experienced over the past few decades. But it is also far too soon to form a complete picture of what that "new normal" looks like.

Of course, how the world got to this moment is clearer. The now "old" normal was defined by an aggressively growing China and a monetarily loose US Federal Reserve. The two were intertwined to a degree. The Fed was reacting to the deflationary pressures brought on by the reduction in manufacturing employment. China was encouraging a surge in its manufacturing base. Meanwhile, the emerging world—largely reliant on commodity exports—was benefiting on all sides. A weak dollar inflated global commodity prices while surging Chinese demand worked to push prices higher as well. This "dual stimuli" propelled the world through the beginning of the 21st century.

The dual stimuli set the stage for the "normal" of the beginning of the 21st century—the awkward interaction of a booming global economy and a transitioning US economy. As manufacturing jobs were offshored and then automated, the US economy found ways to cope. First, it used the housing boom and then the shale oil and gas revolution. Both required the highly paid, low-skilled labor critical to inflating America's bubbles. Now that the bubbles have popped, the question lingers as to where the next low-skill employment boom will occur.

The question for the Chinese economy is whether it is transitioning (to a consumer-driven economy with expanding services) or faltering (due to excessive leverage and inadequate financial structures). Either way, the demand for raw materials is unlikely to be as robust as it was in previous periods. This spells trouble for much of the emerging world, and will shape much of the after normal one.

Also troubling is the monetary pivot taking place in the United States. Leading up to and following the financial crisis, US monetary policy was highly accommodative. This pushed the dollar down and commodity prices higher. However, as the Fed began to taper its QE strategy, the dollar strengthened. The Fed ended the dual stimuli and left the world in an unfamiliar position: without China *and* without the Fed.

Some observers see the current headwinds as transitory. The view the Fed appears to hold. But there is also the less hopeful view of secular stagnation. Secular stagnation, if true, would hold that growth is going to be slow for an extended period of time and that monetary authorities will have little ability to jolt their economies out of it.

To a degree, no one has seen this before. There are certainly correlations to be drawn with different points in recent economic history (which always rhymes), but there has never been an investment boom like China circa the turn of the 21st century. The post-World War II US could be pointed to as a parallel, but the scales are wildly different. And when one followed directly after the other, the growth was unfathomable.

China has taken this chance to become more involved in the global economy, either through engaging with Western institutions or creating similar, seemingly parallel ones. With its "One

Belt, One Road" initiative, China is attempting to regain its historical position in global affairs and economics. This takes investment in other countries, and that takes institutions and capital. The Asian Infrastructure and Investment Bank is one such structure. It will play a crucial role in the development and potential success of China's economic plans.

China has also gained a place as an official reserve currency. The People's Bank of China has recently begun to allow the RMB to move more in line with market forces. In terms of institutions and currency, the after normal, transitional spot we find ourselves in today, is a test of whether or not China has the ability to be a viable alternative to the West. This has yet to be seen. But China is certainly attempting to create alternatives to the longstanding Western structures.

Those countries lucky enough to fall within the shadow of Chinese demand have, until recently, grown rapidly. A new global middle class has appeared. Their demand for goods and services was purported to be the next wave of global growth. But many of the new emerging middle class are reliant on the "old" Chinese growth model. Few, if any, are well equipped to prosper from the "new" Chinese growth model. This is a disconcerting prospect. At least for the time being, the simple, commodity-driven growth of the past is no longer viable. Whether or not the emerging middle class was a side effect of a commodity bubble has yet to be seen. But the after normal economy rewards commodity driven growth far less than the "normal" economy did.

For the US economy, after normal involves a rapidly changing economy and a Fed with an impossible task. America is in the midst of a demographic shift. Technology is rapidly altering the skills needed to compete in a transforming job market. Meanwhile, the Fed is attempting to slowly "normalize" its policy without allowing the economy to overheat or fall into a recession.

Because there is now a global workforce, many jobs can be automated or outsourced if wages rise too much. This contestability of labor is keeping wages low, even as unemployment falls. Contestability is one reason the Fed should be concerned about America's own commodity-linked employment. The Yellen Fed's labor market goals should be directly connected to ensuring that the United States has created enough uncontestable jobs for the Fed to further normalize. These uncontestable jobs are the type that will lead to—or at least allow for—future upward wage pressures. Prime examples are the jobs in America created by the shale oil boom and construction jobs during the housing boom.

Technology is usually a good thing. It nearly always enhances our lives and makes us better off. But it has a habit of evolving—sometimes very quickly. Technology can enhance or degrade the usefulness of certain skills, as well as render job experience entirely useless. The digital technology shift of the past couple decades may be far more important than we thought—especially given the low savings rates of boomers and their need to stay involved in the workforce. The pace of technological change may explain, at least in part, why the current recovery has been so poor. Too many people with too few technology skills remain in the workforce. The inability to reach out to the cutting edge of technology may be holding back the US economy.

The Fed has had a hand in creating the current situation. It also has a tremendous amount at stake in getting its policy correct over the next several years. Not simply because its job is to set interest rates and use other monetary policy mechanisms with judiciousness and care, but also because it is coming under increased scrutiny from nearly every angle.

To operate efficiently with unconventional policy at 0%, the Fed has been forced to be transparent in its intentions and thought processes. But this has side effects. Policy transparency from the Federal Reserve allows other central banks to anticipate its actions—and respond accordingly. This arrangement has its benefits and its consequences. One consequence is that the other major central banks are forcing a revaluation of the dollar—whether the Fed likes it or not. By transmitting its policy function, Yellen and the Fed have essentially allowed for the euro and yen to rebalance lower.

Transparency removes the pain point of coordination. It creates the ability to game the system as well. The Fed has tolerated other central banks piggy-backing off its policy transparency for some time. But now it is making it difficult for the Fed to enact its own policy. Although transparency and loose policy coordination are inseparable elements of the present moment, the Fed is rightfully concerned with potential abuse and amplification of its actions by others.

For now, "normality" for the United States does not change too much. Interest rates are likely to remain relatively low for an extended period. This is partially because the US economy could tip near or into recession from only a minor shock but also because the Fed is hyper-vigilant of potential vulnerabilities in the US economy. It is also because after normal interest rates are unlikely to approach the levels of the boomer years without a crisis sparking the rise.

Tipping the United States into a recession would destroy any remaining confidence in the Fed. It would also cause more saber rattling from Congress about using a monetary policy rule. The Fed wields a tremendous amount of economic power in its monetary policy, and there may be some jealousy emanating from the halls of Congress. But creating a rules-based system with checks against deviation may harm the Fed's credibility by showing consistent gaps between the Fed's targets and reality. The after normal Fed has an unenviable task ahead of it.

There is no "new normal," because the normal of the past couple decades was an unsustainable and once-in-several-generations growth. Now this is the after normal with all of its quirks, shocks, and economic volatility. After normal is the hangover after the party. The global economy may figure out how to deal with this. But the Chinese and US economies, as well as the US Federal Reserve, are not there yet. For now, we are simply in the after normal with little certainty in the future path of the global economy or monetary policy.

64583904R00124

Made in the USA
San Bernardino, CA
22 December 2017